DRAW NEAR TO GOD

A Journey of Faith, Hope, and Love

Douglas Mincey

Great One Publishing, LLC

Published by Great One Publishing, LLC
7 Venture Dr. Suite 104-116
Bluffton, SC 29910

ISBN: 978-1-956786-00-2

Printed in the United States of America

CONTENTS

INTRODUCTION

As we embark on this extraordinary journey, let's begin with a light-hearted disclaimer: I crafted this book with the mature Christian in mind. It's for those who have weathered spiritual storms and now yearns to deepen their roots, draw closer to God, and see their lives transformed into masterpieces reflecting His will. If the idea of gaining wisdom, peace, and renewed hope from God's unfathomable love resonates, this book is for you. So, buckle up —we are about to embark on an adventure that promises to be as thrilling as it is enlightening.

"Draw Near to God—A Journey of Faith, Hope, and Love is a tale of divine love, cosmic conflict, and the ultimate triumph of good over evil. It's a narrative transcending time yet deeply relevant to our daily lives. It offers insights into how to live victoriously amidst life's challenges, instilling hope and reassurance in the face of adversity.

Our journey reveals the origins of evil and its impact on humanity, highlighting the battles Christians face and the victories we are poised to claim. Imagine understanding the full extent of our Adversary's tactics and countering them with the wisdom and strength of God's Word. As you don your spiritual armor, you'll discover how to stand firm against the forces of evil that seek to sway your heart from God's enduring love.

Through these pages, you'll encounter the silent yet significant battles of the heart—times of doubt and discouragement where the Enemy whispers lies of defeat. Yet, with each chapter, we'll navigate these challenges, shining God's light into the shadows and rediscovering the joy and strength found in His promises.

At the heart of our story is the victory secured by Christ—a triumph over sin and death, which He shares with us. This victory heralds a new beginning, an invitation to live in the freedom of God's love, embracing our new identity in Christ and the boundless grace He offers.

As we progress, we delve into the profound and transformative work of the Holy Spirit, the Divine Artist, who molds and shapes us into Christ's likeness. This transformation journey is filled with moments of revelation, enlightening and filling us with hope as we become vessels that reflect God's glory.

"Draw Near to God—A Journey of Faith, Hope, and Love" isn't a how-to manual; this journey is about finding rest in the Lord.

So, get ready to be inspired, to challenge the status quo of your spiritual walk, and to embrace the spiritual wisdom that God has in store for you.

Glory to God!

1

EXPOSING OUR ADVERSARY:

THE SOUL'S NEMESIS

The Origin of Evil: The Celestial Realms

The origin of evil, a concept that has puzzled theologians and Believers alike, is deeply rooted in the biblical narrative. It takes us back to a time before the Earth, to the heart of Heaven itself, where Lucifer, an angel of unmatched beauty and wisdom, was stationed. But what led to his fall? What lessons can we learn from this? Ezekiel 28:14-17 portrays him as the anointed cherub, adorned with every precious stone, perfect in his ways until he harbored iniquity. While not naming Lucifer directly, this passage has been traditionally interpreted as describing his fall, providing insights into the nature of pride and rebellion. What if we could unravel the mysteries of this celestial drama?

The story of Lucifer's fall is a potent illustration of how pride can lead to one's downfall. He was not content with his position and sought to ascend above the stars of God, as depicted in Isaiah 14:12-15. His heart, lifted by his beauty and corrupted by his splendor, led to his desire to become like the Most High. This story parallels many real-world situations where individuals, blinded by their achievements or status, begin to foster a sense of entitlement and invincibility, leading them away from humility and gratitude. Can we not see echoes of this in our own lives?

The concept of free will, a gift from God, plays a crucial role in understanding the origin of evil. God created angels and humans with the ability to choose, reflecting His desire for genuine relationships rather than forced obedience. Lucifer's choice to rebel against God marks the first exercise of this free will in a direction contrary to God's goodness. This pivotal moment introduces the concept of moral choice into the fabric of creation, setting the stage for the cosmic battle between good and evil, and highlighting the profound responsibility that comes with our freedom to choose. Are we not the architects of our own destiny?

The introduction of evil into the world is not just a celestial event but resonates with everyday life and the human condition. Just as Lucifer chose pride over humility, humans continually face moral choices that shape their lives and the world around them. The biblical narrative, with its timeless wisdom, provides the origins of evil and reflects human nature and the constant struggle between the higher self and base desires, offering a lens through which we can understand our own moral dilemmas.

Evil is not an abstract concept in this cosmic drama but a reality that influences individual lives and global events. The story of Lucifer's fall from grace serves as a stark reminder of the consequences of pride and rebellion. It also provides a framework for understanding the presence of evil in the world, not as an independent force but as the result of beings, angelic or human, choosing to act contrary to God's will.

As we delve into the biblical origins of evil, we must view them as ancient texts and stories that continue to inform, guide, and challenge us daily. They serve as a mirror reflecting our own choices and the universal struggle between light and darkness. The biblical account of Lucifer's fall is not just a story but a grand narrative that teaches us about the dangers of pride and the importance of humility, reminding us that our choices have consequences that reach far beyond our immediate perception.

Hell's Misunderstood Purpose

The concept of Hell, as initially intended in biblical Scripture, was not crafted for humanity but for Satan and his rebellious angels. This fundamental understanding stems from Matthew 25:41, where Jesus explicitly states, "Then He will say to those on his left, 'Depart from me, you who are cursed, into the eternal fire prepared for the devil and his angels.'" This Scripture underscores Hell's original purpose: a final, eternal judgment for celestial beings who defied God's sovereignty.

The rebellion of Satan, once a luminary angel known as Lucifer, marks the inception of sin and rebellion against the divine order. Isaiah 14:12-15 details his fall from grace, driven by pride and the desire to ascend above his Creator. This narrative not only chronicles the origin of evil but also sets the stage for the creation of Hell — a realm designated for those who, like Lucifer, choose defiance over submission to God's rule.

Hell's intended purpose is further illustrated in 2 Peter 2:4, "For if God did not spare angels when they sinned, but sent them to hell, putting them in chains of darkness to be held for judgment..." This passage reinforces the notion that Hell was designed as a place of judgment and punishment for fallen angels, highlighting the severity of their rebellion and the justice of God.

In contemporary times, Hell's relevance extends beyond its original intent, touching on human accountability and the afterlife. The transition from Hell's angelic purpose to its human implications reflects the extension of divine justice from celestial beings to humanity. Humans, endowed with free will similar to angels, face the consequences of their choices, particularly the rejection of God's grace and path to salvation. This shift underscores the seriousness of our moral decisions and the need to consider our actions' eternal consequences.

The misconceptions surrounding Hell stem from its portrayal as a place of arbitrary punishment. However, biblical teachings clarify that Hell is a manifestation of divine justice, paralleling the consequences faced by Satan and his followers. The existence of Hell emphasizes the gravity of sin and the profound need for redemption, urging individuals to reflect on their spiritual state and the eternal implications of their choices.

As we navigate through life, the concept of Hell serves as a sober reminder of the ultimate separation from God's presence — the source of all goodness and life. This understanding calls for a heartfelt examination of one's beliefs and actions, aligning with biblical teachings and the redemption offered through Jesus Christ.

Delving deeper into Hell's biblical context, its transition from a place intended for fallen angels to a consequence for unrepentant humanity becomes evident. This shift underlines the universal principles of justice and free will bestowed upon all God's creatures, including humans. The rich man and Lazarus parable, found in Luke 16:19-31, serves as a sad narrative illustrating the stark realities of the afterlife and the enduring consequences of earthly choices in alignment or opposition to God's commands.

The narrative of Hell in human context accentuates not a God of impulse but a God of order and justice, mirroring the judgment initially designated for the rebellious angels. Just as Jude 1:6 states, "And the angels who did not keep their positions of authority but abandoned their proper dwelling—these he has kept in darkness, bound with everlasting chains for judgment on the great Day," humans too, face judgment based on their adherence or resistance to divine guidance.

The relevance of Hell today can be understood through the lens of divine justice, emphasizing that it is a direct response to the rejection of God's grace and mercy offered through Jesus Christ. John 3:18 clarifies this, saying, "Whoever believes in Him is not condemned, but whoever does not believe stands condemned already because they have not believed in the name of God's one and only Son." Here, the eternal fate of individuals hinges on their response to the Gospel, highlighting the just nature of God's judgment.

Misconceptions about Hell often arise from a misunderstanding of God's character—viewing Him as punitive rather than just. However, Scriptures like Romans

6:23 remind us, "For the wages of sin is death, but the gift of God is eternal life in Christ Jesus our Lord." This verse captures the dual realities of divine justice and mercy, presenting Hell as a rightful consequence of sin while offering salvation through Christ as the pathway to avoid this outcome.

Hell, therefore, extends beyond medieval imagery of fire and brimstone to represent a profound spiritual reality — the definitive separation from God's presence, which is the essence of true life and joy. It serves as a reminder for individuals to earnestly seek reconciliation with God, embracing the salvation offered through Christ to avoid the fate initially intended for Satan and his angels.

In the culmination of biblical teachings about Hell, Revelation 20:11-15 presents the final judgment scene, where their deeds and faith in Christ determine the destination of souls. This apocalyptic vision underscores Hell's role within divine justice, emphasizing that, like the fallen angels, humans too are accountable before God. The lake of fire, mentioned as the second death, signifies the ultimate consequence for those separated from God, devoid of His eternal light and love.

This depiction aligns with the foundational purpose of Hell, extending the theme of divine retribution beyond the angelic realm to encompass all creation. Revelation 21:8

further delineates the fate awaiting those who live in defiance of God's laws, underlining the seriousness with which God views sin and rebellion. Yet, within this sobering portrayal lies the enduring promise of redemption and the avoidance of Hell through faith in Jesus, as articulated in Acts 4:12: "Salvation is found in no one else, for there is no other name under heaven given to mankind by which we must be saved."

These biblical truths intricately tie the modern relevance of Hell, challenging prevailing misconceptions and inviting a deeper understanding of God's nature.

Hell is not an expression of divine cruelty but a testament to the reality of God's justice, mirrored against His boundless mercy. It reminds us of the sanctity of moral choice and the profound consequences of our spiritual allegiances.

To address contemporary misunderstandings, we must articulate that Hell underscores not God's eagerness to punish but His unwavering commitment to uphold moral and spiritual order. The existence of Hell serves as a clarion call to humanity, urging a reflection on the life we lead and the choices we make in light of eternity. It propels a meaningful dialogue about faith, repentance, and the transformative power of God's love offered through the sacrifice of Jesus Christ.

In the fabric of everyday life, Hell's doctrinal truth compels us to live with an awareness of our ultimate accountability and the transient nature of earthly existence. It prompts individuals to evaluate their priorities, relationships, and spiritual well-being, fostering decisions anchored in eternal perspectives rather than fleeting worldly concerns.

Conclusively, Hell, as initially intended for Satan and his followers, stands as a stark reminder of the cosmic conflict between good and evil, extending a profound lesson to humanity about the gravity of our choices and the scope of divine justice. This exploration invites Believers and skeptics alike to confront their misconceptions, understand Hell's proper biblical context, and embrace God's redemptive path through Jesus Christ — a path leading away from destruction and towards everlasting life.

This comprehensive reflection aims not to incite fear but to instill understanding, guiding souls toward the light of God's truth and the hope found in Christ, thereby circumventing the tragic destiny once destined solely for the fallen.

The Spread of Celestial Evil to Earth

In continuing to explore evil's origins, the narrative shifts from the celestial realms to the earthly domain, illustrating how the fallout from Lucifer's rebellion impacts humanity. The infamous encounter in the Garden of Eden, where Satan embodies the serpent and introduces sin to the human race, marks the transition. Genesis 3:1-6 recounts the subtle deception that led Adam and Eve to disobey God, a pivotal moment that echoes Lucifer's fall from grace. While simple, this story encapsulates the profound truth about temptation, free will, and the consequences of our choices.

The serpent's approach to Eve in the garden underscores the insidious nature of temptation. It often begins with a question or doubt about God's word and His goodness—similar to the doubts that may have sparked Lucifer's rebellion. Such tactics reflect everyday experiences, where doubts and misleading questions lead individuals away from their moral centers. This scenario illustrates the ongoing battle between truth and deception, a core theme in understanding the origin of evil.

Furthermore, the immediate consequences of Adam and Eve's actions, detailed in Genesis 3:16-24, mirror the broader cosmic consequences of Lucifer's rebellion. Just as Heaven cast out Lucifer, Adam and Eve faced expulsion from Eden, introducing physical and spiritual death into the world. This narrative serves as a poignant reminder of the far-reaching effects of our actions, emphasizing the biblical theme that sin separates us from God, disrupts harmony, and introduces chaos into the created order.

The fall of humanity is critical to understanding the origin of evil because it demonstrates how Lucifer, now Satan, extended his rebellion against God to the human realm. It underscores the interconnectedness of all creation and the ripple effects of sin from the individual to the cosmic level. The biblical portrayal of this event lays the groundwork for understanding human suffering, moral decay, and the pervasive nature of sin, all stemming from the initial act of disobedience.

In everyday life, the story of the fall is a metaphor for the human condition. At some point, each person faces their own "Garden of Eden" moment, standing at the crossroads between obedience and rebellion, truth and deception. The consequences of these choices reflect the ongoing struggle between good and evil, light and darkness, that began with Lucifer's fall.

This segment of the biblical narrative, rich in symbolism and meaning, explains the presence of evil in the world and is a roadmap for navigating the complexities of life with wisdom and discernment. It invites reflection on personal responsibility, the importance of adherence to divine principles, and the constant need for vigilance against the subtle encroachments of evil in daily life.

As we delve deeper into the origins and implications of evil, the biblical stories transition from ancient history to contemporary relevance, offering timeless insights into human nature, moral decision-making, and the ultimate quest for redemption.

Living the Universal Struggle in the Modern World

As we conclude our exploration of the origins of evil, the narrative broadens to encompass the universal struggle between good and evil, a theme that resonates through biblical history and into our modern lives. The biblical account transitions from the individual sins of Lucifer and Adam to the systemic spread of evil throughout human history, as documented from Genesis to Revelation. This progression illustrates the pervasive nature of sin and the unfolding of God's redemptive plan.

The spread of evil after the fall is rapid and far-reaching, affecting every aspect of human existence. Cain's murder of Abel (Genesis 4:1-8) marks the first act of violence, a tragic testament to how sin begets further sin, leading to cycles of violence, betrayal, and corruption. Today's world mirrors this pattern, with greed, envy, and hatred leading to conflicts, broken relationships, and societal breakdowns. The biblical narrative acts as a mirror, reflecting the dark aspects of the human heart and the catastrophic consequences of turning away from God.

However, the story does not end with the spread of evil; it also introduces the concept of divine justice and mercy. The Flood (Genesis 6:5-8), while a judgment against humanity's wickedness, also signifies God's sorrow over sin and His desire to cleanse and restore. This theme of redemption is a silver lining that runs through the fabric of Scripture, offering hope amidst the darkness. It reflects the everyday experience of failing and falling and the possibility of forgiveness, renewal, and a second chance.

The biblical journey through the origins and consequences of evil ultimately leads to the promise of a Savior, Jesus Christ, who comes to address the root of evil by conquering sin and death (John 3:16). This ultimate act of love and sacrifice offers a solution to the problem of evil, providing a way back to God through faith and repentance. It encapsulates the Christian message of hope and the promise of restoration, resonating with the human longing for peace, justice, and love.

In this light, the origin of evil, as depicted in the Bible, transcends historical or theological curiosity. It becomes a framework for understanding the human condition, our moral struggles, and the hope that lies beyond our failures. While ancient, the stories of Lucifer, Adam, and Eve speak to the contemporary issues of pride, temptation, and the consequences of our choices.

Understanding the biblical origins of evil equips us to navigate the complexities of life with a deeper awareness of the spiritual dimensions that underpin our existence. It calls us to reflect on our lives, recognize the subtle ways sin can infiltrate, and embrace the transformative power of God's grace.

In tracing the enigmatic path of evil's origin, we've ventured from celestial realms to the present-day manifestations of pride and rebellion, understanding that the battle against our adversary is both ancient and ongoing. The narrative, rich with symbolic significance, not only demystifies the inception of sin but also serves as a stark reminder of the subtleties of temptation and the ever-present danger of falling from grace. As we move forward, equipped with the wisdom gleaned from these ancient texts, let us remain vigilant, guarding our souls against Satan's insidious tactics of discouragement and standing firm in the light of truth and righteousness.

2

DISCOURAGEMENT:

SATAN'S SILENT WEAPON

Satan's Role in Our Struggles

This chapter delves into the insidious ways in which Satan employs discouragement as a weapon to weaken our bond with God. He instills doubts and fears, making us feel isolated and inadequate. However, by recognizing this strategy, we can fortify our faith, deepen our connection with God, and find solace and strength in Him, even amidst life's most daunting challenges.

From the beginning, Satan has been the master of deception, twisting the truth to suit his purposes. Consider the Garden of Eden: he twisted God's words to make Eve doubt (Genesis 3:1-13). Satan suggested that God was withholding something good from her, planting the first seeds of doubt regarding God's character and intentions.

This age-old tactic, causing us to question God's words and His goodness, remains one of Satan's favorites.

Fast forward to Jesus' time in the wilderness, where Satan tempted Him by manipulating Scripture, trying to induce doubt and self-reliance (Matthew 4:1-11). Jesus' responses provide the perfect example of countering lies with the truth of God's Word. These stories from the Bible show us that Satan's tactics have not changed; he still aims to make us doubt God's Word, His Love, and our Identity.

Let's bring this into today's context with real-life examples. Consider the common scenario of a Christian facing a severe illness. Satan can use this situation to whisper lies: "If God loved you, why are you suffering?" Here, he's using his old tactic of questioning God's love and goodness. As demonstrated by Jesus, the antidote is to cling to the truths of Scripture, affirming God's love even in suffering, echoing Job's unwavering faith despite his trials.

Another modern example is the feeling of isolation or loneliness in the digital age. Satan uses these feelings to convince us that we are alone, that nobody cares, and even God is distant. This deception directly attacks the truth that God is always with us (Matthew 28:20). By recognizing this deception, individuals can counteract feelings of isolation by seeking Christian fellowship and immersing themselves in the truths of God's eternal presence and care.

Satan's strategies today often involve distorting truths, fostering doubts, and encouraging negative thoughts, just as he did in the past. However, our response can still be the same: grounded in Scripture, prayer, and community. Ephesians 6:10-18 tells us to put on the whole armor of God to stand against the devil's schemes. This is not a battle we fight alone but one we face together as a community of Believers.

Understanding Satan's historical deceptions helps us identify his modern-day strategies. Satan doesn't have new tricks; he uses the old ones in new settings. Knowing this, we can be vigilant, stay grounded in God's truth, and support each other in faith.

Real-life examples underscore the relevance of our spiritual armor. They remind us that while the settings may change, the battle does not. Our victory lies in our response – turning to God, affirming His truth, and refusing to stand alone.

So, what does all this mean?

By recognizing Satan as our unmasked adversary, we can confront his deceptive strategies in our current struggles, countering them with the timeless truth of God's Word. This is not just a theoretical concept but a practical tool for daily use. The more you understand Satan's tactics, the better equipped you are to resist them.

The Root of Discouragement

Discouragement often seeps into our lives when our reality falls short of our expectations. This emotional chasm can stem from personal setbacks, societal pressures, or unfulfilled dreams, creating a fertile ground for doubt and despair. Understanding these roots is essential for spiritual and emotional healing.

In the Scripture, we find Moses, a figure synonymous with faith and leadership, yet not immune to discouragement. Leading the Israelites out of Egypt presented Moses with daunting challenges, including criticism, overwhelming responsibilities, and personal insecurities. His story, particularly when he felt inadequate and overwhelmed, as depicted in Exodus chapters 3 and 4, mirrors our own experiences when faced with insurmountable tasks or harsh criticism. Moses' initial hesitance and self-doubt upon God's call at the burning bush reveal a profound truth: even the mightiest among us can falter under unrealistic expectations – whether imposed by others or ourselves.

Unmet expectations often lead to discouragement. We envision our lives, careers, or relationships unfolding in specific ways, and when reality diverges, we feel lost and disillusioned. The parable of the Prodigal Son

(Luke 15:11-32) echoes this sentiment. The younger son's expectation of a fulfilling life away from home crumbles, leading to profound discouragement. Yet, this story also teaches us the redemptive power of returning to our foundational beliefs and values when life doesn't go as planned.

Another source of discouragement is the comparison trap. In the age of social media, it's increasingly easy to compare our behind-the-scenes struggles with others' highlight reels, leading to feelings of inadequacy and despair. The biblical account of Leah and Rachel's rivalry, detailed in Genesis 29 and 30, exemplifies the toxicity of comparison. Despite her blessings, Leah's constant comparison to her sister showcases how comparison can distort our perception of God's gifts, leading to unnecessary heartache and discontent.

Moreover, personal failures and mistakes can deeply discourage us, making us feel unworthy of love, success, or happiness. Peter's denial of Christ, a moment of profound personal failure, illustrates this point vividly. Yet, Peter's story didn't end with his denial. Jesus' forgiveness and reinstatement of Peter as a pillar of the Church, as described in (John 21:15-17), reminds us that our failures are not the end but opportunities for grace and growth.

The practical steps to combat discouragement begin with acknowledging our feelings without judgment. Just as David poured out his soul to God in the Psalms, we, too, can find solace in expressing our struggles and disappointments. Developing a gratitude practice can also shift our focus from what we lack to what we possess, fostering a sense of contentment and reducing the sting of unmet expectations and comparisons.

Additionally, setting realistic goals and celebrating small victories can help mitigate feelings of failure and inadequacy. Just as Joshua set stones to commemorate crossing the Jordan River (Joshua 4:1-14), we can create tangible reminders of our progress and God's faithfulness.

In engaging with these biblical stories and practical steps, we find that the root of discouragement is not a sign of weakness but a common human experience that, when addressed with honesty and faith, can lead to profound personal growth and spiritual renewal. By understanding the roots of our discouragement, we can start to untangle the complex emotions and thoughts that lead us away from God and toward despair. In doing so, we align ourselves more closely with God's truth and love, our ultimate sources of encouragement and strength.

Shining God's Light in Health Trials

In health and faith, modern Christians face various challenges that can lead to significant discouragement. From unexpected diagnoses to prolonged battles with chronic conditions, the journey through illness is often fraught with fear, uncertainty, and spiritual questioning. Yet, within the pages of the Bible, we find narratives that not only mirror our struggles but also offer profound insights and guidance. One such story is King Hezekiah's severe illness, a narrative rich with lessons for facing modern health crises.

King Hezekiah's story, detailed in 2 Kings 20:1-5, begins with a dire situation. The king falls seriously ill, and Isaiah, the prophet, brings him a message from the Lord: "Put your house in order because you are going to die; you will not recover." This stark declaration from God is a moment that many can relate to—a life-altering diagnosis, a conversation that shifts one's world axis in a matter of seconds. Hezekiah's reaction to this devastating news is deeply human; he turns his face to the wall and prays to the Lord, recounting his faithful service and weeping bitterly.

The intensity of Hezekiah's response resonates with anyone who has faced a similar health scare. The feeling of life slipping through one's fingers, the reflection on past actions and deeds, and the desperate appeal to God for more time are experiences many can understand. This moment in Hezekiah's life teaches us the importance of turning to God in our darkest hours, laying bare our fears, achievements, and the desires of our hearts. It's a reminder that our relationship with God becomes a source of strength and solace in the face of health crises.

What is remarkable about Hezekiah's story is not just his fervent prayer but the immediate response from God. Before Isaiah had even left the middle court, the word of the Lord came to him, saying, "Go back and tell Hezekiah... I have heard your prayer and seen your tears; I will heal you." This swift answer from God is a testament to the power of prayer and the intimate relationship Hezekiah had cultivated with the Lord. It demonstrates that in times of illness, our prayers are not in vain; they reach the ears of a compassionate and responsive God.

The practical lessons from Hezekiah's experience are manifold. Firstly, it highlights the value of a life lived in faithful service to God. Hezekiah's recounting of his dedication reminds us that our actions and heart posture toward God matter, influencing our earthly lives and our dialogues with God in moments of crisis.

Secondly, Hezekiah's story teaches us about humility and vulnerability in prayer. In modern times, where self-sufficiency is often prized, admitting our fears and pleading for divine intervention can feel like an admission of defeat. However, Hezekiah's life encourages us to humble ourselves in God's presence and make our requests known.

Additionally, the narrative underscores the importance of community and godly counsel during health challenges. Isaiah, a trusted prophet and advisor, plays a crucial role in Hezekiah's story, serving as the bearer of dire news and divine promise. In contemporary settings, this translates to the value of having supportive, faith-filled individuals around us—be they pastors, friends, or family members—who can offer biblical counsel, pray with us, and help us navigate the complex emotions and decisions accompanying health issues.

Moreover, Hezekiah's healing prompts us to recognize and celebrate the miraculous, whether it comes as a gradual improvement, a sudden change in prognosis, or the strength to endure ongoing challenges. While modern medicine provides many avenues for healing, Hezekiah's story reminds us of the ultimate source of our health and life, encouraging us to maintain a posture of gratitude and recognition of God's hand in our recovery and well-being.

As we reflect on King Hezekiah's illness and recovery, consider how his response to a health crisis mirrors or differs from yours. What can you learn from his direct appeal to God, his recounting of his faithfulness, and his reception of God's merciful response? How might his story influence how you approach God in your health-related fear and uncertainty?

Hezekiah's narrative is a powerful beacon for those navigating the murky waters of health scares and medical uncertainties. It teaches us to confront our vulnerabilities with faith, to seek solace and strength in our relationship with God, and to remember that our cries and tears are never unnoticed by the Lord.

Discouragement in Ministry

Serving in ministry is like a rollercoaster, full of ups and downs. It's similar to Apostle Paul's life: he spread the Gospel and performed miracles but faced jail, shipwrecks, and harsh criticism. His tough times, feeling alone and challenged, are something many of us understand when we serve in our communities or churches. This shared experience, even after thousands of years, reminds us that feeling down in our service isn't about failing but a natural part of helping others.

In the realm of ministry, discouragement often seeps in subtly. It might start with unmet expectations – maybe a community project you've poured your heart into sees little participation, or a sermon you've prepared diligently doesn't seem to resonate as expected. Consider the parable of the sower Jesus shared (Matthew 13:1-23). Not all seeds fell on good soil; similarly, not all our efforts will yield visible fruit. This reality, however challenging, is a reminder that the success of our labors isn't always ours to see.

Criticism often acts as a source of discouragement, a reality that hasn't changed since the time of the Apostle Paul. He faced severe critique when the Corinthians questioned his authority and motives (2 Corinthians 10:10-18). This situation mirrors the challenges faced by today's church leaders, volunteers, and missionaries. They, like Paul, may encounter misunderstandings or harsh judgments, not just from outsiders but sometimes from within their church communities. For example, a modern church leader might introduce a new outreach program to help the community but only face skepticism or resistance from congregation members who resist change. This criticism resembles Paul's experience despite his pure intentions and miraculous works.

Burnout represents another facet of discouragement in ministry, stemming from continuous giving without adequate personal replenishment. The story of Elijah, particularly after his victory on Mount Carmel (1 Kings 19:4-8), is a vivid depiction of burnout. Despite his triumphant showdown, he flees into the wilderness, overwhelmed and pleading for his life to end. It's a poignant reminder that profound valleys of exhaustion and despair can follow spiritual victories.

Furthermore, loneliness or lack of recognition can weigh heavily on ministry members. Moses felt this deeply when he cried out to God, feeling the weight of leading the Israelites alone (Numbers 11:14-17). Such feeling echoes in the lives of many who serve in various capacities today – from pastors and mission workers to Sunday school teachers and church volunteers – who may feel their efforts are unseen or underappreciated.

How can one navigate these choppy waters of ministry-related discouragement? First, anchoring in the truth of God's Word and promises is essential. Just as Paul centered his response to criticism and hardship on the foundation of Christ's strength and his divine calling, we should root our identity and worth in who we are in Christ, not in the fluctuating opinions of others or the immediate results of our efforts.

Practicing self-care is also crucial. Elijah's story didn't end in despair; God met him in exhaustion, providing rest and sustenance before directing him back to his mission (1 Kings 19:5-8). This divine intervention underscores the importance of physical, emotional, and spiritual self-care in sustaining our ministry efforts. Regular periods of rest, prayer, fellowship, and personal study can replenish our spirits and prevent burnout.

Moreover, embracing community support plays a vital role in overcoming discouragement. Moses was advised to delegate responsibilities to capable leaders, distributing the burden among others (Exodus 18:17-23). Similarly, seeking support through mentorship, prayer groups, or simply sharing the load with trustworthy team members can alleviate loneliness and overwhelm.

Lastly, seeing things the way God does can change our outlook. It's important to remember that the seeds we plant in our work might not sprout right away – some may even grow after we can't see them anymore. Maintaining this perspective is where faith and patience come in, just like with the mustard seed Jesus talks about in Matthew 13:31-32. Even the tiniest seed can grow into a big tree. In the same way, the little things we do in our ministry can make a big difference, even if we don't see it happen ourselves.

Discouragement in Relationships

Relationships form the bedrock of our daily lives, yet they can often lead to feelings of discouragement when misunderstandings, disappointments, or conflicts arise.

Reflecting on biblical stories can provide us with guidance and comfort during these times.

Consider the story of Job, who experienced extreme suffering and loss. His friends, attempting to offer comfort, blame him for his misfortunes (Job 2:11-13; Job 4:1-9). Our experiences mirror this when we seek support from friends and instead encounter criticism or misunderstanding.

It's like reaching out for a helping hand and instead being pushed away, intensifying our feelings of isolation and discouragement.

Then there's David and King Saul. Initially, Saul adored David, but soon, his feelings turned to jealousy, leading to attempts on David's life (1 Samuel 18:6-11; 1 Samuel 19:1-2). This story is reminiscent of workplace scenarios where a once-supportive colleague or boss turns against us, fueled by envy or miscommunication, leaving us feeling betrayed and undervalued.

The tale of Joseph and his brothers offers a powerful example of forgiveness and reconciliation (Genesis 45:1-15; Genesis 50:20-21). After being sold into slavery by his family, Joseph endures years of hardship but eventually forgives his brothers. This story relates closely to family disputes where past hurts, and misunderstandings cause estrangements. It encourages us to seek healing by addressing old wounds and moving toward forgiveness.

These biblical narratives reflect common scenarios in our personal and professional lives. They teach us about the complexity of human emotions and relationships and offer hope for healing and reconciliation. Whether dealing with a misunderstanding with a friend, facing jealousy from a colleague, or navigating family tensions, these stories remind us that we're not alone in our struggles. They also encourage us to strive for understanding, seek reconciliation where possible, and extend forgiveness just as we hope to receive it.

In navigating the ups and downs of relationships, we can draw comfort and guidance from these timeless lessons, applying their wisdom to our modern-day challenges. If you're facing a situation discouraging you, consider which of these stories resonates with your experience. What steps can you take to address the issue, guided by the patience, forgiveness, and wisdom illustrated in these biblical examples?

Exploring the stealthy battleground where discouragement aims to sever our ties with the Divine, we've uncovered Satan's schemes of sowing doubt and isolation. Armed with awareness, our journey strengthens our faith, fortifies our bond with God, and empowers us to seek refuge in Him during trials.

As we close this chapter, let us carry forward this shield of knowledge, preparing ourselves for the ongoing spiritual warfare that challenges our souls. Understanding this is crucial as we prepare for challenges testing our spiritual identity.

3

UNDER SIEGE:

THE BATTLE FOR YOUR SOUL

Understanding Spiritual Warfare in Everyday Life

S piritual warfare is an all-encompassing, invisible conflict that impacts our day-to-day existence, threading through our thoughts, decisions, and interactions. While unseen, this battle is vividly described in the scriptures, showcasing a timeless struggle between divine truths and Satan's deceptive tactics. Satan operates behind the scenes to thwart God's plans and lead His Servants astray.

Following his dramatic victory on Mount Carmel, Elijah's narrative is a moving example of this spiritual warfare (1 Kings 19:1-18). After achieving a significant triumph, showcasing God's power through fire from Heaven, Elijah encounters a severe spiritual and emotional downturn due to Jezebel's death threats. This shift from victory to vulnerability underscores a typical strategy of Satan:

attacking during moments of weakness. Despite witnessing God's power firsthand, Elijah succumbs to fear, illustrating how easily we can forget God's past faithfulness when faced with new threats. Today, this mirrors our experiences when, after spiritual highs or personal achievements, we unexpectedly encounter threats or challenges that plunge us into fear or doubt. These moments reveal Satan's tactic of using our vulnerabilities to instill fear, aiming to erase the memory of God's previous deliverance and faithfulness.

Elijah's response—running away and wishing for death—reflects a human tendency to isolate and despair when overwhelmed. Yet, God's gentle approach, providing sustenance and rest before questioning Elijah, teaches us the importance of self-care and seeking God in our lowest points. Modern parallels are found in seeking help during mental health struggles, taking time for rest and reflection, and remembering to turn to God and trusted community members when facing life's "Jezebels."

In the story of Joseph, we witness a different dimension of spiritual warfare. His brothers sell him into slavery, and he later faces unjust imprisonment, marking his journey with injustice and hardship (Genesis 37:23-28, Genesis 39:1-23). Yet, each trial, orchestrated by human hands, has Satan's fingerprints all over it, aiming to destroy Joseph's Spirit and God-given destiny. Despite this, Joseph's steadfastness, integrity, and forgiveness in the face of betrayal and false accusations highlight the strength that comes from faith and moral conviction. His ability to resist Potiphar's wife's advances, interpret dreams under God's guidance, and manage Egypt's resources wisely shows how maintaining integrity and utilizing God-given talents can lead to the promotion and fulfillment of divine purposes, even in a foreign land.

Today, Joseph's story resonates with anyone who has faced betrayal, false accusations, or workplace harassment. It reminds us that a more profound spiritual battle often lies behind personal and professional attacks. The lesson for modern Believers is clear: maintaining integrity, practicing forgiveness, and trusting in God's overarching plan can lead to eventual vindication and purpose realization, even from the depths of a metaphorical pit.

Understanding spiritual warfare, as depicted in the lives of Elijah and Joseph, requires recognizing that there is often a spiritual Adversary behind our fears, challenges, and persecutions. However, these stories also reinforce the unwavering faith, resilience, and divine guidance that allowed Elijah and Joseph to overcome the tactics meant to derail them. Their stories provide a blueprint for triumph in spiritual warfare, inspiring us to stand firm in our faith and reliance on God. This emphasis on their triumph can instill a sense of hope and determination in us, knowing that victory is possible even in the face of spiritual battles.

As we delve deeper into these narratives and their modern-day implications, we equip ourselves with the knowledge and strategies to navigate the complexities of life while engaged in an ongoing spiritual battle for our souls. By understanding and applying the lessons from Elijah's and Joseph's experiences, we learn to recognize Satan's subtle workings and to stand firm in our faith, fortified by God's grace and strength. Focusing on the lessons learned can provide guidance and direction, helping us navigate our own spiritual battles.

Continuing from our initial look into spiritual warfare through Elijah and Joseph, we now focus on other biblical figures who faced similar trials. How can these ancient stories be relevant to our modern lives? The answer lies in the universal nature of human experiences and the timeless wisdom of these narratives. This shows us that this battle is historical, deeply personal, and relevant today. Their experiences, though from a different time, mirror our own struggles, offering us a profound sense of connection and understanding in our own spiritual battles.

Take a look at Job's story. Known for his unwavering righteousness, Job faces severe trials not because of any wrongdoing but as part of a larger cosmic bet between

Satan and God (Job 1:6-12). This situation uncovers a significant aspect of spiritual warfare: our pain and loss might sometimes be part of a more extensive spiritual test. Like Job, modern Believers might face unexplained hardships that challenge their faith. The key takeaway is not the presence of suffering but steadfast faith during suffering, defying Satan's expectations and proving our genuine trust in God's plan.

Then there's Peter – a devoted follower who denies Jesus three times out of fear (Luke 22:54-62). But later, Peter is restored and even strengthened in his faith (John 21:15-19). This swing from confidence to fear and back to faith shows us that spiritual warfare often targets our fears and insecurities. In today's context, this could relate to the fear of judgment or rejection from others for our beliefs. Peter's story teaches us that failure isn't final. It's an opportunity for growth and a reminder that Jesus is ready to restore and use us despite our shortcomings.

In today's fast-paced world, pressures at work or in our social circles can mirror Peter's experience at the courtyard – moments when standing for our faith could invite criticism or isolation. Yet, recalling Peter's restoration can encourage us to face our fears, knowing that our identity and worth are secured in Christ, not in public approval.

These biblical narratives underscore that behind every fear, loss, and challenge, Satan spearheads an underlying spiritual battle. Satan aims to shake our faith and distract us from our divine calling. However, they also highlight that victory lies not in our own strength or efforts but in persistent faith, honest repentance, and, most importantly, divine grace. It is through God's grace and strength that we can overcome the tactics of the spiritual Adversary, and this reliance on God is the key to our triumph in spiritual warfare.

The stories of Job and Peter show that we fight spiritual warfare in the mundane aspects of life: how we deal with personal setbacks, respond to misunderstandings, and stand firm in faith when conforming seems easier. They teach us that our response to life's trials can affirm our faith or reveal our vulnerabilities. However, in every case, they offer opportunities for profound growth and deeper reliance on God, reminding us that we can find hope and strength even in the midst of spiritual warfare, instilling in us a sense of optimism and resilience.

As you navigate your daily life, facing professional challenges, personal dilemmas, or societal pressures, remember the source behind these trials – Satan's schemes. This knowledge equips you to respond not with despair but with faith-driven resilience. Approach your challenges with a renewed perspective by learning from Job's steadfastness and Peter's restoration. See them as arenas for demonstrating your faith, integrity, and the transformative power of God's love.

In this ongoing journey through spiritual warfare, it is essential to move beyond mere recognition of the battle to engage in it actively with the tools God provides. This engagement unfolds not with fear or defeat but with the assurance that God's presence and guidance accompany us, and Christ promises us eventual victory.

As we advance, we'll explore how to practically arm ourselves with God's given resources, ensuring we're not just survivors but overcomers in this continuous spiritual conflict. Continue to the next section for practical insights into utilizing the whole armor of God to navigate and conquer the challenges posed by spiritual warfare in our daily lives.

Dressing for Battle: Employing the Full Armor of God

As we continue, imagine the difference between getting dressed and gearing up for battle. In the physical world, soldiers don armor for protection and readiness, each piece serving a vital purpose. For Christians, this concept translates into spiritual armor, a divine provision for our daily battles against unseen forces. Just as armor shields warriors and enhances their capabilities, spiritual armor equips Believers with strength, protection, and resilience. Each garment is for covering and empowering us to stand firm.

Because the landscape of spiritual warfare that Believers navigate is complex and often treacherous, featuring valleys of despair and hills of adversity, the Apostle Paul offers profound guidance to the early Saints:

"Finally, be strong in the Lord and in His mighty power. Put on the full armor of God so that you can take your stand against the Devil's schemes. For our struggle is not against flesh and blood, but against the rulers, against the authorities, against the powers of this dark world, and against the spiritual forces of evil in the heavenly realms. Therefore, put on the full armor of God so that when the day of evil comes, you may be able to stand your ground, and after you have done everything, to stand. Stand firm then, with the belt of truth buckled around your waist, with the breastplate of righteousness in place, and with your feet fitted with the readiness that comes from the gospel of peace. In addition to all this, take up the shield of faith, with which you can extinguish all the flaming arrows of the evil one. Take the helmet of salvation and the sword of the Spirit, which is the word of God (Ephesians 6:10-17)."

Amid life's battles, the indwelling Holy Spirit empowers, guides, and protects us. We are vessels, not the source of power, but the carriers of His divine presence. This perspective shifts the focus from our strength or ability to the transformative power of the Spirit within us.

Let's look at the story of David and Goliath as an example (1 Samuel 17:38-51). David, a young shepherd, faced a giant not in his strength but with faith in God's deliverance. It was the Spirit's empowerment that gave him the confidence to confront Goliath. Today, we face 'giants'—challenges at work, personal struggles, and social pressures. Like David, when we face these giants, it's not our prowess but the Holy Spirit within us that equips us with the courage, wisdom, and strength to overcome.

The "Belt of Truth" and the "Breastplate of Righteousness" are not mere metaphors but signify the essence of living a life aligned with God's Word and His righteousness, guided by the Spirit. In a world filled with deception and moral ambiguity, the Spirit leads us into all truth (John 16:13), helping us navigate decisions, relationships, and conflicts with integrity and moral clarity, much like Daniel in the lion's den who remained steadfast in his devotion despite the threat of death (Daniel 6:13-23).

The "Shoes of Peace" in the Gospel remind us of the peace that surpasses all understanding, which guards our hearts and minds (Philippians 4:7). This peace, a fruit of the Spirit, enables us to stand firm in chaotic circumstances, offering serenity that can defuse conflicts, reconcile relationships, and lead others to the Prince of Peace.

Taking up the "Shield of Faith," we can deflect the enemy's fiery darts—doubts, fears, accusations. Just as Peter walked on water when he fixed his eyes on Jesus (Matthew 14:29), so does the faith given by the Spirit enable us to rise above life's turbulent waves and not sink into despair.

The "Helmet of Salvation" protects our minds from the onslaught of negative thoughts and doubts about our identity and worth. Remembering that God has saved, chosen, and loved us—reaffirmed through the Spirit's assurance in our hearts—fortifies us against the lies of unworthiness and condemnation.

Lastly, the "Sword of the Spirit," the Word of God, becomes active and alive within us through the Holy Spirit. When Satan tempted Jesus, He countered each temptation with Scripture (Matthew 4:1-11). Likewise, the Spirit prompts us to wield God's Word as a defensive tool and an offensive weapon that pierces darkness, reveals truth, and brings liberation.

As Paul concludes in Ephesians 6:18, our spiritual armor is complemented and activated by prayer: "And pray in the Spirit on all occasions with all kinds of prayers and requests. With this in mind, be alert and always pray for all the Lord's people." Praying in the Spirit is our direct line to God, a means to stay spiritually alert, intercede for others, and remain in tune with God's will. Through prayer, we maintain our connection to the divine power source, allowing the Holy Spirit to work through us more effectively.

In embracing this truth—the Holy Spirit as our protector and guide—we find a defense against spiritual warfare and victory in our daily lives. We are not just surviving; we are thriving, advancing, and overcoming by the power of the Spirit within us. Let this encourage you: in Christ and with the indwelling Spirit, you possess equipment, empowerment, and eternal safeguarding. Walk in this truth and let the Holy Spirit manifest God's glorious victory in and through you daily.

Battles of the Flesh: The Samson Syndrome

Transitioning from understanding the full Armor of God, we delve into the life of Samson, who exemplifies the struggle against fleshly desires and the tangible consequences when such battles are lost. Samson's story, detailed in Judges 13-16, offers profound insights into the nature of temptation and the crucial need for spiritual vigilance.

From birth, the Nazirite vow set Samson apart, granting him extraordinary strength not for his glory but to serve as an instrument of Israel's deliverance from the Philistines. Yet, despite his divine calling and formidable strength, his life was marred by a series of compromises and surrenders to fleshly desires, especially in his dealings with Delilah (Judges 16:4-21). Samson's downfall was not sudden but a gradual erosion of integrity and purpose, underscored by repeated neglect of his spiritual commitments.

In modern terms, Samson's vulnerabilities mirror Christians' everyday temptations—in the allure of unhealthy relationships, pursuing personal gratification over God's directives, or neglecting spiritual duties for fleeting pleasures. The story underscores that physical strength, intellectual ability, or even spiritual gifts are insufficient without the governance of God's Spirit and adherence to His commands.

The seduction by Delilah is not merely a historical narrative but a cautionary tale about the subtlety of temptation. It often arrives cloaked in appeal and familiarity, challenging resistance without the Spirit's help. Delilah's persistence highlights how temptation frequently revisits, each weakening resolve until resistance crumbles. In contemporary settings, this could manifest in persistent challenges to our moral standards, repeated exposures to compromising situations, or the gradual desensitization to sin due to constant societal pressure.

Samson's eventual capture and humiliation are a stark reminder of the long-term consequences of yielding to fleshly weaknesses. However, Samson's story does not end in defeat. In his final moments, he turns back to God in prayer, and God momentarily restores his strength to fulfill his initial calling (Judges 16:28-30). This moment of redemption underscores the principle that, despite past failures, returning to God in genuine repentance can restore purpose and power.

As Believers transition from the concept of the Armor of God to confronting personal temptations, Samson's narrative encourages us to maintain our spiritual guard, continually relying on the Holy Spirit's guidance rather than our strength or wisdom. The lessons from Samson's life compel us to reflect on our vulnerabilities, to identify the 'Delilahs' in our lives, and to reinforce our spiritual commitments to withstand and overcome temptations.

Continuing our journey through understanding spiritual warfare and its manifestation in the temptation of the flesh, we will further explore practical strategies to safeguard against succumbing to fleshly desires, reinforcing the need for spiritual armor in these personal battles.

We now delve deeper into preventative measures, the power of accountability, and the continuous reliance on the Holy Spirit to navigate and triumph over the temptations that challenge our spiritual walk and destiny.

Building upon our reflections on the story of Samson and the broader theme of spiritual warfare, particularly in resisting fleshly desires, we arrive at critical strategies for maintaining our spiritual integrity. Samson's narrative, culminating in his final act of repentance and redemption, illustrates the consequences of giving in to temptation and the power of returning to God despite past failures.

The lessons from Samson's experiences are invaluable in contemporary Christian life. Every Believer is in a personal battle against the temptations that assail our flesh and Spirit. We fight these battles through the daily decisions we make, the relationships we cultivate, and the priorities we set. The essence of overcoming these temptations lies in our strength, continuous reliance on the Holy Spirit, and adherence to God's Word.

The concept of accountability emerges as a vital tool in safeguarding against the lure of fleshly desires. Just as Samson might have benefited from godly counsel and accountability, modern Believers are encouraged to seek and maintain relationships with fellow Christians who provide support, guidance, and correction when necessary. This accountability can be practical involvement in small group settings, mentorship relationships, or a transparent friendship where spiritual challenges and victories are shared.

Moreover, daily spiritual disciplines such as prayer, scripture reading, and worship are not mere religious rituals but essential practices that strengthen our inner being, align us with God's will, and fortify us against the seduction of sinful desires. Integrating these practices into our everyday lives ensures that we are constantly nourished by the truth, reminded of our identity in Christ, and empowered by the Holy Spirit to overcome temptations.

The power of the Holy Spirit within us is the cornerstone of our defense against fleshly desires. It is He who convicts, guides, and empowers us to live lives that are pleasing to God. Yielding to the Spirit's promptings allows us to navigate life's challenges and temptations with wisdom and discernment. In moments of weakness, the gentle whisper of the Spirit can guide us back to the path of righteousness, much like the quiet reflection that led Samson to his final act of faith.

As we conclude this exploration into the temptation of the flesh and the story of Samson, it's crucial to embrace the truth that, while we are mere vessels, we carry within us the indomitable Spirit of God. This divine presence is our protector, guide, and strength in times of weakness. Ephesians 6:18 reminds us to "pray in the Spirit on all occasions with all kinds of prayers and requests." Through prayerful reliance on the Holy Spirit, we find the strength to resist temptation and the grace to recover from falls.

Let this be a source of encouragement: our battles against fleshly desires are not fought alone or insurmountable. With the Holy Spirit as our guide and protector, we can navigate the complexities and challenges of life while maintaining our spiritual integrity. In every decision, temptation, and moment of weakness, let us turn to Him, allowing His power to work through our yielded hearts.

In embracing the Holy Spirit's role in our lives, we become not only survivors of spiritual battles but victors in Christ, demonstrating His power and love to a world in desperate need of His transformative grace.

Distorted Reflections: Losing God's Image to Sin

Transitioning from the intricate discussions of spiritual warfare and the personal battles each Believer faces, we now approach the culminating segment of our journey—understanding how sin, a pervasive and destructive force, impacts our lives and relationships, distorting the image of God within us. This final exploration aims to delve into the profound consequences of sin and the necessity of reconciliation with God.

Romans 7:18-20, expressed by Apostle Paul, resonates deeply within the collective Believer's experience: "For I know that good itself does not dwell in me, that is, in my sinful nature. For I have the desire to do what is good, but I cannot carry it out. For I do not do the good I want to do, but the evil I do not want to do—this I keep on doing." Although

Paul speaks in the first person, his struggle mirrors a universal battle, emphasizing that sin's pervasive influence tarnishes even our best efforts without Christ steering our lives.

Sin's impact extends beyond mere actions; it infiltrates the very essence of our communication with God, often leaving Believers feeling distant, unworthy, and hypocritical. The parable of the Pharisee and the Tax Collector (Luke 18:9-14) underscores this point; it contrasts the self-righteous prayer of the Pharisee with the humble, penitent prayer of the tax collector. Jesus commends the tax collector's attitude, highlighting that recognizing one's sinfulness and dependency on God's mercy is the first step towards genuine communion with the Creator.

For many, this sense of unworthiness and hypocrisy can become a significant barrier to prayer and spiritual growth. The feelings of inadequacy can be so overwhelming that Believers may withdraw from prayer, assuming their unworthiness disqualifies them from God's attention or grace. The enemy's lies that the blood of Jesus is insufficient to cleanse us thoroughly from our sins further compound this.

We can take practical steps to navigate this spiritual dilemma. Acknowledging and confessing serve as the pillars for overcoming feelings of unworthiness and hypocrisy. As 1 John 1:9 assures, "If we confess our sins, He is faithful and just and will forgive us our sins and purify us from all unrighteousness." Confession and the sincere acceptance of God's forgiveness begin dismantling the barriers sin erects between us and God.

Moreover, fostering an environment of transparency within a faith community can be profoundly liberating. Sharing one's struggles and victories diminishes the power of hidden sins. It strengthens the bonds of fellowship as we realize the commonality of our struggles and the shared triumphs in Christ.

When trapped by sin, the fruits of the Spirit — love, joy, peace, patience, kindness, goodness, faithfulness, gentleness, and self-control — often appear as distant ideals. Yet, Galatians 5:22-23 portrays them not as self-achieved merits but as natural results of a life guided by the Spirit. This portrayal marks a transition from self-reliance to dependence on God, shifting the focus from our incapacity to His sovereign power to transform and renew.

Continuing from our exploration of the profound challenges Believers face in sin, the story of King David offers a poignant illustration of sin's devastating impact and the collateral damage it can cause. David, a man after God's own heart, was not immune to the destructive power of sin. His narrative, particularly his adultery with Bathsheba and the subsequent murder of her husband Uriah, encapsulates the deep pain and far-reaching consequences of his actions, as seen in 2 Samuel 11-12.

David's sin led to immediate and long-term suffering for himself and his entire household. The child born from his adultery died, a direct consequence of his actions. Beyond this immediate punishment, David faced rebellion within his own family, a result foretold by the prophet Nathan as a direct fallout from his sins. The sequence of events following his transgression—Absalom's revolt, Amnon's sin against Tamar, and the ongoing strife within his kingdom—highlight how one moment of moral failure can unravel into a series of tragic events, affecting not just the sinner but generations to follow.

Psalm 51 vividly portrays the personal agony David experienced, showing his plea for God's mercy and a clean heart. His remorse went beyond mere regret for getting caught; it reflected a profound recognition of how his sin had marred his relationship with God, distorted his moral compass, and caused indescribable pain to others." For I know my transgressions and my sin is always before me. Against you, you only, have I sinned and done what is evil in your sight..." (Psalm 51:3-4). David's story shows that although repentant hearts can be sure of God's forgiveness, the earthly consequences of our actions may still unfold, causing pain and heartache.

The ripple effects of sin can similarly be seen and felt in our lives today. Choices made in moments of weakness can lead to broken relationships, lost trust, and many personal and communal pains. David's narrative is a stark reminder to guard our steps and seek God's wisdom in every decision. Yet, it also reminds us that no situation is beyond God's redemption. Healing and restoration can begin through genuine repentance and turning back to God.

The practical steps toward recovery from sin's impact involve acknowledging our wrongdoings, seeking forgiveness from those we've hurt, and making amends where possible. It requires a commitment to change, underpinned by daily prayer, scripture study, and the support of a faith community. These actions don't undo the past but pave the way for a new chapter marked by God's grace and guidance.

The journey from acknowledging our sins to experiencing the fullness of God's redemptive grace is profound. It reaffirms that, despite the depths of our failures, the heights of Christ's victory on the cross are infinitely greater. Armed with this truth, we step into the next chapter not as defeated sinners but as redeemed individuals, walking in the victory and freedom bestowed upon us through Christ's ultimate sacrifice.

4

THE FINAL VERDICT:

NO CONDEMNATION IN CHRIST

Life After 2 Corinthians 5:17

Transitioning from the spiritual battles that Believers endure, which can be characterized by doubts about our faith, purpose, and worth, and assaults on our integrity, we embark on a transformative journey in Christ. This journey signifies a shift from enduring darkness to embracing profound changes, highlighting survival and thriving in our new life.

At the heart of our transformation lies the profound declaration in 2 Corinthians 5:17: "Therefore, if anyone is in Christ, the new creation has come: The old has gone, the new is here!" This Scripture is not just a verse but a personal invitation to a life immersed in God's grace, redeeming our past and anchoring our future in Christ's victory. The new creation identity is not a distant concept but a profound spiritual reality we can experience when we accept Christ. It is a new way of being, a new perspective, and a new purpose that we are called to live out.

Deep understanding and embrace of our new identity are guided by Ephesians 4:22-24: "You were taught, with regard to your former way of life, to put off your old self, which is being corrupted by its deceitful desires; to be made new in the attitude of your minds; and to put on the new self, created to be like God in true righteousness and holiness." This passage encourages us to discard our former ways, characterized by selfishness, pride, and disobedience, and to clothe ourselves in a new self modeled after God's righteousness and holiness.

Romans 6:4-6 speaks directly to our new creation identity, illustrating our baptism into Christ's death and resurrection as the foundation for walking in the newness of life. The newness of life refers to the spiritual rebirth and transformation that occurs when we accept Christ. We are called to live out a new way of being, perspective, and purpose. "We were therefore buried with Him through baptism into death in order that, just as Christ was raised from the dead through the glory of the Father, we too may live a new life. For if we have been united with Him in a death like His, we will certainly also be united with Him in a resurrection like His." This baptism symbolizes our break from sin's dominion, ushering us into a life marked by victory and divine purpose.

1 Peter 2:9-12 shines a spotlight on our mission as God's chosen people: "But you are a chosen people, a royal priesthood, a holy nation, God's special possession, that you may declare the praises of Him who called you out of darkness into his wonderful light." This Scripture is a divine commission that underscores our unique role in reflecting God's goodness in a world entangled in darkness. It reminds us of our calling to live out the kingdom's virtues and shine as beacons of hope and transformation.

The conversion of Saul to Paul provides a powerful illustration of being made a new creation. Initially known for his zealous persecution of the early church, Paul's dramatic encounter with the risen Christ on the road to Damascus (Acts 9:1-19) catalyzed an extraordinary transformation. From a fierce opponent, Paul emerged as one of the most influential proponents of the Christian faith, dedicating his life to spreading the Gospel. Paul's journey from Saul to Paul embodies the essence of transformation in Christ—a life once marked by opposition to the Gospel becoming a testament to the transformative power of God's redemptive Love. His writings and missionary journeys underscore the reality that we are indeed new creations in Christ, called to a life of purpose, service, and witness to the grace that has transformed us.

Living as new creations in Christ is not a burden but a source of immense joy and fulfillment. It's a daily commitment to embody the renewal we've experienced, sharing the story of transformation and hope with the world. In doing so, we bear witness to the grace of God that reshapes our existence and impacts the world, reflecting the fullness of life promised in Christ. This journey is a testament to the joy and fulfillment of embracing our new identity daily, guided by Paul's life-changing example and the enduring truths of Scripture.

Moreover, our new creation identity is not just about us but also influences our community engagement. Understanding that we are not just random beings but 'God's handiwork, created in Christ Jesus to do good works, which God prepared in advance for us to do' (Ephesians 2:10) propels us into action. We are part of God's grand plan, not just here by chance. Whether through our vocations, volunteer efforts, or simply in daily interactions, we seek to reflect God's love and grace, serving as His valued Ambassadors in every sphere of influence.

Living out this identity also means facing and overcoming challenges with a perspective anchored in victory. While struggles and temptations, such as doubt, fear, or the lure of worldly pleasures, remain a reality, our approach transforms these trials. James 1:2-4 encourages us to consider it pure joy when we face trials of many kinds, knowing that testing our faith produces perseverance. This perspective shift doesn't minimize the difficulties but frames them within the larger narrative of growth, maturity, and reliance on God's strength.

Much like Paul's, our stories are not just personal narratives but living epistles read by all who encounter us. They point beyond our transformation to the Gospel's transformative power. Our lives, actions, and words should all witness the change that Christ has brought in us, inviting others to experience the same transformation.

Christ's Liberation: Freed from Sin's Penalty

Transitioning from embracing our new identity in Christ, we delve into the profound truth of our liberation through Christ's sacrifice. "Christ's Liberation: Freed from Sin's Penalty" underscores the significant aspect of our faith: the deliverance from sin's ultimate consequence, inviting us into a life of freedom and hope anchored in Scripture.

At the core of the Gospel is a transformative truth that redefines our existence and eternal fate. Romans 6:23 encapsulates this pivotal message: "For the wages of sin is death, but the free gift of God is eternal life in Christ Jesus our

Lord." Herein lies the contrast between the outcome of sin and the extraordinary grace bestowed upon us through Jesus Christ. Sin's wage, death, is counteracted by the life-giving gift of eternal life through faith in Christ.

Rejoice, for Romans 8:1 offers us a powerful reassurance: "Therefore, there is now no condemnation for those who are in Christ Jesus." This statement liberates us from the weight of condemnation, marking us as redeemed and fully absolved through Christ's love and sacrifice. It's the bedrock of our confidence and joy in the Christian walk. Let this truth sink in, and feel the weight of condemnation lifted off your shoulders.

A biblical account that exemplifies liberation from sin's penalty is the story of the woman caught in adultery (John 8:1-11). Presented before Jesus, she faced the physical penalty for her actions under the law and public shame and condemnation. Yet, Jesus' response, "Let any one of you who is without sin be the first to throw a stone at her," and His subsequent forgiveness, "Then neither do I condemn you... Go now and leave your life of sin," highlights the essence of Christ's mission – to offer grace and liberation to those bound by the penalty of their sins.

Living in the light of Romans 6:23 and Romans 8:1 invites us to embody the grace and freedom we've received. The story of the woman caught in adultery in John 8:1-11 not only showcases Jesus's refusal to condemn but also His call to a life transformed: "Go now and leave your life of sin." This moment encapsulates the call to each of us, free from condemnation, to live lives that reflect our changed status.

The transformation brought about by Christ's sacrifice is profound and comprehensive. It involves an external change in our actions and relationships and an internal renewal of our minds and spirit. We transition from viewing ourselves as condemned sinners to redeemed children of God, fully accepted and loved. This shift influences our relationship with God, enabling us to approach Him with the confidence of children rather than the fear of judgment.

Externally, our liberation manifests in our relationships and actions. Freed from the penalty of our sins, we gain the power to forgive others as others forgave us, pursue righteousness in our actions, and act as peacemakers and bearers of grace in our communities.

The grace we've received becomes the grace we give, reflecting Christ's character in our daily interactions.

Christ's Liberation: Freed from Sin's Power

This next section delves into the transformative aspect of salvation, a journey that pardons us from sin's power and liberates us from its dominating grip. The Apostle Paul illuminates this truth in Romans 6:22, "But now you are free from the power of sin and have become slaves of God..." This profound declaration forms the bedrock of our transformation, leading us to a life empowered by the Spirit and liberated from sin's tyranny.

The essence of our freedom from sin's power is intricately woven through the narrative of Scripture, illuminating the full scope of Christ's victory on the cross. Paul elaborates on this freedom in Romans 7 and 8, emphasizing that Believers are no longer subject to sin's enslaving power. This liberation is not a mere theological concept but a lived reality enabled by the new life of the Spirit within us. "For you did not receive a spirit that makes you a slave again to fear, but you received the Spirit of sonship. And by Him, we cry, 'Abba, Father'" (Romans 8:15). The Spirit's indwelling marks our adoption into God's family and equips us with the power to overcome sin's lure.

The narrative of the Israelites' exodus from Egypt and their journey toward the Promised Land is a biblical metaphor for our liberation from sin's power. Just as God led His people out of slavery, He led us out of sin's bondage and into a life marked by freedom and holiness. The Israelites walking on dry land through the Red Sea, as their pursuers washed away, mirrors our baptism into Christ's death and resurrection—we leave behind the old life of sin and step into a new life in Christ.

In everyday life, this freedom influences how we approach challenges, temptations, and our pursuit of holiness. It's the difference between fighting battles in our strength versus leaning on the Spirit's power. For example, a person fighting habitual sin might notice that, although temptation continues, their compulsive draw to sin weakens as they actively follow the Spirit's guidance. This change doesn't imply a journey free from struggle; instead, it highlights that their newfound strength and resilience originate from dedicating themselves as "slaves of God" to righteousness.

Furthermore, this liberation propels us into active service and worship, motivated by gratitude for our salvation. Freed from sin's power, we reflect God's will and purpose for our lives through our actions and choices. Whether volunteering at a local shelter, reconciling strained relationships, or simply living with integrity in our workplaces, these become outpourings of the life-changing grace we've experienced. These acts of service and worship are not attempts to earn God's favor but responses to the love and freedom we've received.

Living in the freedom Christ won enables us to embody the Kingdom of God's virtues tangibly. The Spirit transforms our lives into beacons of light, guiding others toward the same freedom we've received. This transformation involves more than just leading a moral life; it involves actively participating in God's work of restoration and reconciliation. Walking in the Spirit, we find ourselves loving more deeply, serving more selflessly, and speaking truth more boldly—actions that reflect God's heart to the world around us.

The narrative of Paul's missionary journeys, detailed throughout the Acts of the Apostles, exemplifies the potential impact of a life freed from sin's power. Paul, transformed by his encounter with Christ, dedicated his life to spreading the Gospel, founding churches, and nurturing the early Christian community. His letters to these churches, filled with theological insights and practical advice, continue to guide and inspire Believers today. Paul's life underscores that freedom from sin's power is foundational to effective ministry and enduring spiritual legacy.

As we conclude this exploration of "Christ's Liberation: Freed from Sin's Power," let us carry forward the profound truths and practical insights gleaned from Paul's teachings in Romans. May our lives, continually being transformed by the Spirit, testify to the liberating power of the Gospel. Let us move forward with a renewed commitment to live in this freedom, not as an end but as a means to love, serve, and glorify God in everything we do.

The Divine DNA: Love as the Blueprint

Transitioning from our deep dive into being "Freed From the Power of Sin," where we explored the liberating truth of our victory over sin through Christ, we now venture into understanding the essence and impact of divine love. This shift moves us from the battleground of sin to the embrace of an unconditional love that defines our existence.

At the heart of God's character is love—a love so profound and unfathomable that it serves as the foundation of His relationship with us. 1 John 4:8 succinctly captures this truth: "...for God is love." This simple yet profound statement reveals that love isn't just an attribute of God; it is His very essence. This love initiated the world's creation, promised redemption to fallen humanity, and accomplished salvation through the cross of Christ.

1 Corinthians 13:4-7 describes love's characteristics, which, in essence, describe God's nature toward us: "Love is patient, love is kind. It does not envy, it does not boast, it is not proud. It does not dishonor others; it is not self-seeking, is not easily angered, and keeps no record of wrongs. Love does not delight in evil but rejoices with the truth. It always protects, always trusts, always hopes, always perseveres." In these verses, Paul delineates the attributes of love fully

embodied in God's actions toward humanity. This love is patient with our weaknesses, kind in our failures, rejoicing in truth, and persevering through our struggles.

The story of Balaam, found in Numbers 22, intriguingly showcases God's sovereign will and His protective love over His people. Despite Balaam's initial intent to curse Israel at the directive of Balak, God intervenes, turning the curse into a blessing (Numbers 22:12, 22-35). This narrative highlights God's unwavering commitment to His Covenant People, a testament to His unconditional love that seeks our good even when we are unaware of the dangers that lurk. God's intervention in Balaam's journey underscores that His love is proactive, often shielding us from harm and guiding us back to His will, irrespective of our plans or understanding.

Expanding on the expression of God's love in our lives, Romans 5:8 beautifully encapsulates the depth of God's love: "But God demonstrates His own love for us in this: While we were still sinners, Christ died for us." This scripture vividly illustrates that God's love isn't contingent upon our righteousness or moral standing. Instead, it's a love that reaches out to us in our most broken state, offering redemption and restoration. Christ's sacrifice is the ultimate demonstration of love's power to transcend conditions, inviting us into a life of freedom and fellowship with God.

In our daily lives, the unconditional nature of God's love challenges us to extend the same grace and forgiveness to others. A practical example of this appears in family relationships. Just as a mother's love for her child remains steadfast through mistakes or failures, we should love those around us unconditionally, support and uplift them in their struggles, and celebrate their victories as if they were our own. This kind of love—patient, kind, and enduring—can heal wounds, bridge divides, and restore relationships, mirroring the reconciling work of Christ in our lives.

Moreover, understanding and embracing God's unconditional love empowers us to face our shortcomings and challenges with hope and resilience. Knowing we are loved by God, not because of what we do, but because of who He is, offers us a secure foundation to build our lives. It encourages us to pursue personal growth and holiness, not out of fear of losing His love, but in response to the love we have already received.

The communal aspect of God's love calls us into a shared experience and expression of love within the body of Christ. John 13:34-35 commands us to love one another as Christ has loved us, indicating that our love for each other is a primary witness to the world of Jesus' presence and power in our lives. This mutual love among Believers is a source of strength and encouragement, a beacon of hope, and a signpost to the kingdom of God for those outside the faith. How we care for, forgive, and bear with one another in love can draw others toward the transformative love of Christ.

Missionally, God's unconditional love propels us to engage with the world in meaningful and transformative ways. It motivates us to act justly, love mercy, and walk humbly with our God (Micah 6:8), reaching out to the marginalized, the oppressed, and the lost with the same love we have received. This love is not passive; it seeks out the lost sheep, it binds up the brokenhearted, and it brings justice to the oppressed. Our mission, fueled by God's love, becomes one of restoration and reconciliation, embodying the kingdom of God in every act of service and every word of truth spoken in love.

A relatable example of this love in action appears in the countless ways Believers call themselves to serve their communities. Whether it's through volunteering at a local food bank, mentoring at-risk youth, or simply offering a listening ear to a neighbor in distress, these acts of love are practical demonstrations of God's love flowing through us. They embody the love described in 1 Corinthians 13:4-7, revealing patience, kindness, protection, trust, hope, and perseverance in real-world contexts.

Moreover, engaging in these acts of love allows us to witness the Gospel's transformative power firsthand. We see lives changed, not just by the physical or emotional support offered but through the spiritual renewal often accompanying acts of unconditional love. These experiences reinforce our understanding of God's love as a dynamic force that heals, restores, and reconciles.

In conclusion, the journey through "The Nature of God's Love" does not end here but continues each day as we live out the reality of this love in our personal lives, communities, and worldwide. Embracing God's unconditional love challenges us to view every person and every situation through the lens of this love, driving us to action and inspiring us to love more deeply and widely.

Grasping God's Unconditional Love

Having delved into "The Divine DNA: Love as the Blueprint," where we explored the foundational role of love in God's character, we are now poised to uncover further the profound nature of God's Unconditional Love. This next section invites us to discover the depths of a love that is not just a part of God's identity but is also a hidden treasure, constantly present and waiting to transform us. Understanding this love, so essential and foundational to our Christian walk, merits extended discussion.

It's about realizing the breadth and constancy of a love that far surpasses our daily experiences and becomes the bedrock of our faith.

Consider the message of John 3:16: "For God so loved the world that He gave His one and only Son, that whoever believes in Him shall not perish but have eternal life." This biblical verse isn't just about historical events; it's about a profound and boundless love that breaks through all barriers. Imagine someone who offers to take your place in a difficult situation out of sheer love – this barely scratches the surface of what this verse conveys. It's about ultimate sacrifice, where God provided a way for us to have a fulfilling and eternal connection with Him despite our flaws and mistakes.

Then there's 1 John 4:19, "We love because He first loved us." Our ability to love, show compassion, and connect with others is rooted in experiencing God's love. Like a child learning behaviors from their parents, we learn to love from the ultimate source of love – God. In practical terms, it's like finding kindness and compassion within ourselves when we help a stranger or comfort a friend, reflecting the love first shown to us.

Ephesians 2:4-5 also depicts God's love: "But because of his great love for us, God, who is rich in mercy, made us alive with Christ even when we were dead in transgressions—it is by grace you have been saved." Even when we're at our lowest, feeling unworthy and lost, God's love is there to lift us and breathe life into our worn-out souls. Imagine a plant without water for an extended period and then brought back to life from the brink of death – that's a glimpse of what God's love does for us spiritually.

Romans 5:8-10 reveals, "But God demonstrates His own love for us in this: While we were still sinners, Christ died for us." God's love doesn't wait for us to become perfect; He loves us in our imperfections. This love is akin to a parent's unconditional love for their child, regardless of mistakes or misbehavior. God's love is steadfast and unwavering, even when we feel undeserving.

Finally, Psalms 86:15 describes God's endless loving nature: "But you, Lord, are a compassionate and gracious God, slow to anger, abounding in love and faithfulness." This true love portrays God as patient, kind, and ever-faithful, like a lighthouse guiding ships safely to shore. God's love can be seen in those moments of unexpected grace and assistance when we least expect but most need it – a reminder of the steady presence.

These passages offer a powerful yet simple message for anyone seeking a more intimate relationship with God: "Draw near to God, and He will draw near to you...(James 4:8).

In real-life terms, we feel God's presence in moments of loneliness, the strength we find in times of weakness, and the guidance we receive when we're lost. It's about realizing that no matter where we are or what we've done, God's love always reaches out to us.

Living Hope: The Heartbeat of Our Daily Walk

After exploring God's love, we will focus on "Living Hope," born from that love. Anchored in the resurrection of Jesus Christ, this hope offers a vision of a future that surpasses our current reality, providing assurance and molding our daily lives with a perspective aimed at eternity.

At the forefront of our exploration into hope is 1 Peter 1:3-5, a passage that sets the tone for this theme: "Praise be to the God and Father of our Lord Jesus Christ! In His great mercy, He has given us new birth into a living hope through the resurrection of Jesus Christ from the dead, to an inheritance that can never perish, spoil, or fade. This inheritance is kept in heaven for you." This scripture highlights the source of our hope—the resurrection of Jesus Christ—and the nature and outcome of this hope: an imperishable, unspoiled, unfading inheritance kept in heaven for us. This living hope transcends mere temporal aspirations, anchoring us in the promise of a secure and glorious eternal future.

As this passage underscores, Biblical hope is a confident expectation similar to our assurance that Spring follows Winter. It is a hope grounded not in the uncertainty of human circumstances but in the unchangeable character of God and Jesus' ultimate victory over sin and death. This kind of hope infuses our lives with meaning, guiding us through periods of waiting and uncertainty with a steadfast heart and a joyous anticipation of what is to come.

Other scriptures further illuminate this theme. Romans 15:13 blesses us with this prayer: "May the God of hope fill you with all joy and peace as you trust in Him, so that you may overflow with hope by the power of the Holy Spirit." This verse reveals that our hope is not self-generated but is a gift from the God of hope, cultivated within us by the Holy Spirit, leading to an overflow of joy and peace.

The story of Joseph, spanning from Genesis 37 to Genesis 50, exemplifies living hope amidst adversity. Despite being sold into slavery by his brothers, falsely accused, and imprisoned, Joseph's hope in God's promises never waned. His journey from the pit to the palace underscores that biblical hope enables us to see beyond our present trials to God's larger plan of redemption and restoration. Joseph's unwavering hope was not disappointed, as he eventually witnessed the fulfillment of God's dreams, playing a pivotal role in the salvation of his family and many others during a famine.

This living hope manifests in various ways in our everyday lives. It is present in a student's perseverance in working towards a degree, the dedication of individuals serving their communities, and the patience of those enduring hardships while trusting God's faithfulness. Like the assured transition from Winter to Spring, our hope in Christ encourages us to face each day confidently, knowing that our current trials are temporary compared to the eternal joy that awaits us.

Advancing in our exploration of "Living Hope," we delve further into the richness of this theme, emphasizing the eternal perspective that shapes our understanding and expression of hope in our lives.

Colossians 3:1-4 vividly portrays the eternal perspective of our hope, with Paul encouraging Believers to focus their hearts and minds on things above, not earthly things. This directive emphasizes the essence of living in hope: it pushes us to see beyond our current reality to our eternal future in Christ. "For you died, and your life is now hidden with Christ in God. When Christ, who is your life, appears, you will also appear with Him in glory." This passage reminds us that our true life, the one full of hope and promise, is secured with

Christ in God, reaffirming our expectations for a glorious future alongside Him.

This eternal perspective influences how we engage with the world around us. Understanding that our ultimate hope lies in our future resurrection and inheritance in the Kingdom of God shapes our priorities, decisions, and actions. It encourages us to invest in what is eternal—relationships, love, and the spread of the Gospel—rather than in this world's fleeting pleasures or achievements.

The hope we possess is not just for our comfort but also serves as a beacon of light to those who are still searching for meaning and purpose. 2 Corinthians 4:16-18 offers profound insight into this aspect of hope, highlighting that our momentary troubles are achieving for us an eternal glory that far outweighs them all. "So we fix our eyes not on what is seen, but on what is unseen, since what is seen is temporary, but what is unseen is eternal." By focusing on the eternal, we live out a hopeful existence that testifies to the enduring nature of God's kingdom and His promises.

The narrative of Moses choosing to suffer mistreatment with God's people instead of enjoying sin's fleeting pleasures (Hebrews 11:24-26) exemplifies living with an eternal perspective. His vision of the reward—an eternal inheritance with God—drove Moses' decision, far surpassing the temporary benefits of his status in Egypt. His life illustrates how an eternal outlook fosters a willingness to endure present hardships for future glory.

Practically, living hope from an eternal perspective is like choosing integrity over compromise, service over self-interest, or forgiveness over bitterness. It's seen in our daily choices to reflect Christ's love, pursue righteousness, and extend grace, knowing that our actions resonate with eternal significance.

While continuing our exploration of living hope, let's embrace the full spectrum of this theme, from the personal to the cosmic, understanding that our hope in Christ sustains us individually and unites us in shared anticipation of God's final redemption.

The narrative of hope culminates in the promise of new creation—a future where God will restore everything and dwell with His people in perfect harmony. Revelation 21:1-4 paints a vivid picture of this hope realized: "Then I saw a new heaven and a new earth, for the first heaven and the first earth had passed away... He will wipe every tear from their eyes. There will be no more death or mourning or crying or pain, for the old order of things has passed away." This passage offers comfort and a profound hope that transcends our present suffering, anchoring us in the promise of eternal life and joy in God's presence.

This eternal perspective transforms how we live today. It empowers us to face trials with courage, engage with our communities with love, and steward God's creation with care, knowing that what we do in the Lord is not in vain. Our hope in the coming kingdom motivates us to work towards reflecting its values here and now, striving for justice, peace, and reconciliation in a broken world.

Living hope also means being agents of hope to others. Our confident expectation of God's promises enables us to offer support and encouragement to those around us, bearing witness to the hope within us. 1 Peter 3:15 urges us, "But in your hearts revere Christ as Lord. Always be prepared to give an answer to everyone who asks you to give the reason for the hope that you have." Our lives, marked by hope, become testimonies to the faithfulness of God, inviting others to discover the source of our hope.

The story of Abraham, revisited in the context of hope's culmination, offers a model for us. Abraham's journey wasn't just about his faith and the fulfillment of promises in his lifetime but pointed forward to a greater fulfillment in Christ—the ultimate heir through whom all nations would be blessed. Similarly, while personal, our hope is part of a larger story of redemption that encompasses all creation and finds its fulfillment in Christ.

As we conclude our journey through "Living Hope," let us move forward with the conviction that our hope is not baseless or unfounded but secured in the person and work of Jesus Christ. This hope is not just for the future; it invigorates our present, shaping how we live, love, and serve in anticipation of what is yet to come.

May our exploration of hope inspire us to live each day with an eternal perspective, faithfully embodying the hope of the Gospel in a world that longs for redemption. Let us move forward with joy, knowing that our hope in Christ is both the anchor for our souls and the compass for our journey, guiding us toward the glorious future God has promised to all who love Him.

Walking in Grace: The Path to Spiritual Victory

Transitioning from the theme of hope, we turn our attention to "Walking in Grace," recognizing God as the ultimate source of this grace. This section highlights God's grace, deeply anchored in our core beliefs. Ephesians 2:8-10 unfolds the profound mystery of God's grace—a divine kindness so boundless that it transcends human understanding. This passage reminds us that our salvation and lives are not products of our merit but manifestations of God's unfathomable grace. As we delve into this concept, let us explore how God's grace, demonstrated through biblical narratives and mirrored in our everyday lives, compels us to live in gratitude, awe, and deeper communion with our Creator.

The concept of grace is not just a New Testament revelation but woven throughout the biblical narrative. For instance, the Old Testament recounts the story of Noah, where Genesis 6:8 notes, "But Noah found grace in the eyes of the Lord." Here, amidst humanity's widespread corruption, God's grace preserves Noah, a precursor to the saving grace extended to all through Christ. Similarly, in Exodus 33:19, God proclaims to Moses, "I will make all my goodness pass before you, and I will proclaim the name of the Lord before you; and will be gracious to whom I will be gracious." This declaration underscores that grace is a facet of God's character, demonstrating His sovereignty and benevolent will.

In the New Testament, grace becomes even more explicitly connected with Jesus. John 1:17 states, "For the Law was given through Moses; grace and truth came through Jesus Christ." Zacchaeus, a tax collector despised by his community, experiences a transformative encounter with Jesus, leading to his repentance and restitution. Here, grace initiates restoration and change, showcasing how divine kindness leads to authentic, heartfelt transformation, not superficial compliance (Luke 19:1-10).

The parable of the Lost Sheep (Luke 15:3-7) further exemplifies the nature of grace. The shepherd leaves the ninety-nine sheep to find the lost one, rejoicing greatly upon its return. This story parallels God's relentless pursuit of individuals, underscoring that grace is personal and seeks out each of us in our defiance. Like the shepherd's joy over the one sheep, there is "joy in heaven over one sinner who repents" (Luke 15:7).

But grace is not merely about salvation; it's also about how we live out our salvation. Titus 2:11-12 tells us, "For the grace of God has appeared that offers salvation to all people. It teaches us to say 'No' to ungodliness and worldly passions and to live self-controlled, upright, and godly lives in this present age." Here, grace is both the initiator of salvation and the guide for a life transformed by that salvation. It's a source of empowerment that enables us to live lives that reflect God's goodness and righteousness.

In practical terms, understanding grace changes our daily lives and challenges. When confronted with difficulties, rather than despairing, we can remember 2 Corinthians 12:9, where the Lord says, "My grace is sufficient for you, for my power is made perfect in weakness." This assurance empowers Christians to endure hardships, not in their strength but with the strength provided by God's grace.

In essence, God's grace is comprehensive, extending from the initial act of saving faith to the ongoing process of sanctification. It's an unending, unfailing resource available to Believers, transforming our weaknesses into testimonies of divine strength and reflecting our lives on God's Love.

As recipients of this incredible gift, we should respond with gratitude, living lives that not only reflect God's grace but also extend it to others. In doing so, we become examples of God's transformative love and vessels through which others may encounter this life-altering grace.

Extending God's Grace to Others

After delving into how we experience and live out God's grace personally, our journey takes us to the broader application of sharing that grace with others. This step invites us to reflect Christ's love through our actions and relationships, becoming conduits of His grace in the world. It's a shift from internal transformation to outward expression, showing how embodying and extending grace impacts those around us and enriches our spiritual walk.

The Christian life is deeply woven with grace, reflecting God's love and forgiveness. When we show grace to others, we demonstrate Christ living in us, changing lives around us just as God changes ours.

The ultimate example of grace is Jesus Christ. As stated in 1 Peter 3:18, "For Christ also suffered once for sins, the righteous for the unrighteous, that he might bring us to God, being put to death in the flesh but made alive in the spirit." This verse succinctly captures the essence of Christ's sacrifice and the grace it signifies. Christ, the sinless one, suffered for all sins so that we, the unrighteous, could be reconciled to God. This Scripture offers a touching illustration of grace; Jesus took our place and bore our sins, an act of immense love and the epitome of unearned favor.

This principle of grace is central to our faith and should permeate our interactions with others. Consider the parable of the prodigal son (Luke 15:11-32). In this story, a wayward son squanders his inheritance, yet his Father welcomes him with open arms and a celebratory banquet upon his return. This narrative encapsulates the essence of divine grace —unmerited mercy and love, echoing how God welcomes us back into His embrace, regardless of our past transgressions.

The story of the Good Samaritan (Luke 10:30-37) also serves as a powerful example. In this parable, a man is beaten and left on the roadside. While others pass him by, the Samaritan, an unlikely helper, stops to aid the injured man without any expectation of reward. Crossing cultural and societal boundaries, compassion, and grace illustrates the call to extend God's grace to all, regardless of their background or beliefs.

As followers of Christ, we must serve as Ambassadors of grace. Ephesians 4:32 reminds us, "Be kind and compassionate to one another, forgiving each other, just as in Christ God forgave you." This call to action transcends mere words, urging us to manifest grace through our deeds and interactions.

Moreover, extending grace can transform not only the lives of recipients but also our own lives. It involves recognizing everyone's worth and responding with understanding and help without judgment. This behavior glorifies God and makes His love visible in the world.

Now, as Christ's disciples, we are challenged to let our light shine brightly (Matthew 5:16). This means living our lives so that others can see the grace and love of God reflected in our actions. It's about living as a testimony to God's goodness, drawing others to Christ's light through our kindness and mercy. We have the call to embody our faith with boldness and visibility, allowing God's grace to flow through us, illuminating the darkness, and glorifying His name.

Embodying God's grace and allowing our light to shine, we serve as beacons of hope and love in a troubled world. This grace fulfills our divine purpose and honors God's name, drawing others closer to His embrace.

5

SANCTIFICATION:

THE SPIRIT'S ETERNAL MISSION

Unveiling Sanctification: Foundations in Scripture

Every Believer's journey begins and ends with biblical hope—a confident expectation rooted in God's promises. Yet, this hope reaches its fullness only when we grasp the profound concept of sanctification. As we start our quest to gain clarity about this topic, let's heed the counsel of the Apostle Peter to the early Church, a timeless piece of wisdom that rings true for us today: "Always be prepared to give an answer to everyone who asks you to give the reason for the hope that you have..." (1 Peter 3:15). This directive encourages us to be ready to share our faith. It underscores the necessity of understanding the bedrock of our beliefs, among which sanctification stands as a cornerstone.

Sanctification is a term of depth and spiritual significance, often bandied about in Christian discourse. At its core, sanctification entails a divine calling to be "set apart" for God's sacred purposes, embarking on a path toward holiness. It is a transformative process that each Believer undertakes in their quest to mirror the likeness of Christ. The Apostle John highlights this concept through Jesus' prayer in John 17:1: "Sanctify them in the truth... your word is truth." Here, sanctification is illuminated as both a setting apart and a purification, achieved through the truth of God's Word.

The New Testament further clarifies this doctrine through the apostolic teachings, where sanctification is synonymous with holiness. Peter, in his first epistle, exhorts and urges the Believers with these stirring words: "But just as He who called you is holy, so be holy in all you do; for it is written: 'Be holy, because I am holy'" (1 Peter 1:15-16). This call to holiness is not a suggestion but a divine mandate, an echo of the Old Testament commandments, and a reflection of God's unchanging nature.

Sanctification, therefore, is not merely a theological concept to be understood but a lived experience, manifesting through a life consecrated to God and His purposes. It invites us into a life of transformation, where the Word of God acts as both the map and the compass, guiding us toward becoming more like Christ in thought, word, and deed.

As we proceed, let us delve deeper into the Scriptures, exploring the narrative of sanctification as it unfolds from

Genesis to Revelation. We will examine pivotal moments and characters that exemplify this process, understanding that sanctification is a personal and communal experience woven into our individual and collective faith journeys.

The Holy Spirit's Sanctifying Work

Within the narrative arc of the New Testament, the transformation of Saul of Tarsus into the Apostle Paul is a profound demonstration of the sanctifying work of the Holy Spirit. Paul's journey from a fervent persecutor of the church to one of its most pivotal leaders and writers illuminates the transformative power of the Holy Spirit to conform our lives to the likeness of Christ.

Acts 9:1-19 vividly captures the turning point in Paul's life. On the road to Damascus, Saul encounters the risen Christ in a blinding vision, leading to a radical transformation of his heart and mission. This moment marks the beginning of Saul's sanctification process, where the Holy Spirit molds his life to reflect Christ's character and purposes. "Immediately, something like scales fell from Saul's eyes, and he could see again. He got up and was baptized" (Acts 9:18). Baptism here symbolizes Saul's cleansing and dedication to God, a powerful outward sign of an inward grace facilitated by the Holy Spirit.

Paul's writings further underscore the role of the Holy Spirit in sanctification. In his letter to the Galatians, he contrasts the works of the flesh with the fruit of the Spirit, teaching that "the fruit of the Spirit is love, joy, peace, forbearance, kindness, goodness, faithfulness, gentleness and self-control" (Galatians 5:22-23). These virtues reflect the character of Christ and are evidence of the Spirit's sanctifying work in a Believer's life.

To bring this concept into a relatable, everyday context, consider the transformation many experience when they surrender their lives to Christ. An individual might struggle with anger, impatience, or selfishness—traits that are all too common in our human condition. Yet, as they grow in their relationship with God, there's a noticeable shift in their demeanor. Over time, through prayer, scripture reading, and fellowship with other Believers, the Holy Spirit begins to refine their character, replacing those fleshly inclinations with His fruit. Anger gives way to patience, impatience to peace, and selfishness to love. It's a gradual process, often taking place over years, but the change is evident to those around them.

Paul's epistles are replete with warnings and encouragements that point to the Holy Spirit's role in this transformation. For instance, in Ephesians 4:22-24, He urges Believers to "put off your old self... and to put on the new self, created to be like God in true righteousness and holiness." The process of "putting on" the new self is not something Believers can achieve on their strength but is the work of the Holy Spirit, sanctifying them for God's glory.

Paul's life and teachings offer a compelling narrative and theological foundation for understanding the sanctifying work of the Holy Spirit. His transformation from Saul to Paul exemplifies how the Spirit renews our minds, changes our hearts, and empowers us to live lives that reflect Christ. As modern-day Believers, embracing this truth invites us into a journey of transformation, one where the Holy Spirit shapes us into the likeness of Christ, enabling us to impact the world around us with the love and grace of the Gospel.

Sanctification in Action: Living Out the Holy Calling

As we explore the essence of sanctification further, it becomes evident that this divine process is not confined to personal spiritual growth but extends into every facet of our daily lives, illustrating the profound impact of living out our holy calling.

The Apostle Paul, in his letter to the Romans, presents a vivid portrayal of sanctification as a lived experience: "Therefore, I urge you, brothers and sisters, in view of God's mercy, to offer your bodies as a living sacrifice, holy and pleasing to God—this is your true and proper worship" (Romans 12:1). Paul's exhortation moves sanctification beyond the abstract, positioning it as an active, daily offering of oneself to God. This act of offering is not a momentary gesture but a continual posture of worship, a testament to the transformative power of God's grace in shaping lives.

The journey of sanctification also marks the fruits it bears in a Believer's life. Galatians 5:22-23 outlines these fruits: "But the fruit of the Spirit is love, joy, peace, forbearance, kindness, goodness, faithfulness, gentleness and self-control. Each fruit is a tangible expression of sanctification at work, revealing the character of Christ forming within us. As we grow in these virtues, our lives become a living testimony to the sanctifying work of the Spirit, drawing others to the hope we possess.

Moreover, we view the narrative of sanctification through the stories of countless Believers who have walked this path before us. Consider Joseph, who, despite being unjustly sold into slavery and wrongfully imprisoned, remained steadfast in his faith and integrity. His journey from the pit to the pinnacle of Egyptian governance is a powerful testament to sanctification's outworking, demonstrating how God's purposes prevail, even in adversity.

Another poignant example is Esther, whose courage and faith led her to risk everything to save her people. Her story underscores the sanctified life's call to action—standing in the gap for others, guided by wisdom and prayer. Esther's life exemplifies how sanctification involves setting oneself apart for God's redemptive purposes.

These examples, among many others, serve as beacons of hope and encouragement, reminding us that sanctification is a journey we do not walk alone. It is a collective calling to embody the holiness to which we have called ourselves, impacting the world around us. As we navigate this path, let us draw strength from the stories of those who have gone before us and the transformative power of God's Word, continually shaping us into vessels fit for His service.

Weaving Holiness into Community

As we explore the multifaceted nature of sanctification further, we encounter its communal dimension, revealing how individual transformation intricately links to the collective spiritual journey of the church. Sanctification is not an isolated endeavor but a communal process that fosters unity, growth, and mutual support among Believers. This aspect of sanctification reminds us that we are part of a larger body, each member contributing to the whole's sanctity and purpose.

The New Testament church, as depicted in the Acts of the Apostles, serves as a vibrant model for living out sanctification in the community. Acts 2:42-47 describes the early Believers' dedication to the Apostles' teaching, fellowship, breaking of bread, and prayer. Their shared life marked itself by awe, generosity, and a profound unity. This early Christian community exemplified how sanctification weaves through the very fabric of communal life, with each Believer's growth contributing to the collective witness of the church.

This communal aspect of sanctification challenges us to consider how our journey of holiness impacts and enriches the church body. Hebrews 10:24-25 encourages us to "consider how we may spur one another on toward love and good deeds, not giving up meeting together, as some are in the habit of doing, but encouraging one another." Here, we see sanctification as a cooperative venture where Believers call themselves to inspire, support, and uplift one another in their pursuit of holiness.

Moreover, the communal dimension of sanctification extends beyond the confines of the church, influencing the broader society. As Believers live out their holy calling, they become salt and light in the world (Matthew 5:13-16), drawing others towards the Gospel's transformative power. This outward expression of sanctification showcases the kingdom of God in action, where acts of love, justice, and mercy reflect the heart of God to a watching world.

In this tapestry of sanctification, every thread—every Believer's story—adds strength and beauty to the whole, displaying the manifold wisdom of God. As we weave our lives into this communal fabric, let us do so with intentionality and grace, mindful of our role in nurturing the growth and holiness of the church. Through our collective witness, may the world see a vivid picture of the kingdom of God, inviting all into the transformative journey of sanctification.

Reflecting Holiness: The Sanctification of Daniel

In the rich tapestry of biblical narratives that illustrate sanctification, the story of Daniel stands out as a compelling testament to the power of a life dedicated to God. Daniel's journey, characterized by unwavering faith and integrity amidst the challenges of exile and service in a foreign court, exemplifies how sanctification is both a personal commitment and a witness to the surrounding world.

From the onset of his story, Daniel faces a test of his faith and commitment to God's statutes. Daniel 1:8 reveals his resolve: "But Daniel resolved not to defile himself with the royal food and wine." This seemingly simple decision was a profound act of sanctification, setting Daniel apart and marking his life as dedicated to God's purposes. It was a choice that demonstrated his holiness and positioned him as a vessel through which God could work powerfully.

Daniel's sanctification was not merely about personal purity; it had far-reaching implications. God granted Daniel the ability to interpret dreams and visions, which served as a bridge between the kingdoms of the world and the kingdom of heaven. Through Daniel, God revealed His sovereignty over history and kingdoms, showcasing His power to uplift and depose rulers. Thus, Daniel's life became a canvas on which God painted His redemptive plan for the nations, intricately weaving the theme of sanctification throughout the narrative of history.

Furthermore, Daniel's unwavering commitment to prayer, even in the face of potential death in the lions' den (Daniel 6:10-23), underscores the essence of sanctification as a relationship with God that he maintains through faithfulness, prayer, and trust. His deliverance from the lions' den is a powerful demonstration of God's faithfulness to those set apart for Him, reinforcing that sanctification involves trusting God amidst life's most difficult situations.

Daniel's story invites us to reflect on the meaning of sanctification in our own lives. It challenges us to consider how we, like Daniel, can live lives set apart for God's purposes, influencing the world through our faith and integrity. As we navigate the complexities of modern life, let Daniel's example inspire us to hold fast to our convictions, cultivate a vibrant relationship with God, and live out our holy calling, no matter the circumstances. Through such lives of dedication, we continue the legacy of sanctification, bearing witness to God's kingdom and His redemptive work in the world.

God's Grace: Our Sanctified Journey

As we conclude our in-depth exploration of sanctification, let us reflect on each Believer's profound journey guided by the divine grace of the Holy Spirit. The Apostle Paul encapsulates this journey in Philippians 3:13-14, where he shares, "Brothers and sisters, I do not consider myself yet to have taken hold of it. But one thing I do: Forgetting what is behind and straining toward what is ahead, I press on toward the goal to win the prize for which God has called me heavenward in Christ Jesus." This passage highlights the continual nature of our spiritual growth and Paul's relentless pursuit of becoming more like Christ—a goal every Believer shares.

Sanctification is a dynamic and ongoing process. It is not merely about human effort but about divine transformation. Each day, we must lay aside our former ways and embrace the newness of life from the Spirit. This intricate process involves our willing participation and the Holy Spirit's decisive action. As Paul suggests, it requires us to forget what is behind—our past sins, failures, and even past victories—and press toward what lies ahead. This forward-looking mindset keeps us focused on the ultimate prize: full conformity to the image of Christ.

Yet, it is crucial to recognize that while we endeavor to reflect Christ more each day, the full completion of our transformation awaits Christ's return. In this life, we experience incremental victories in holiness, each step marked by the Spirit's sanctifying work. However, only when we see Christ face to face will our sanctification be complete and our redemption fully realized. This future hope does not make our efforts futile but infuses them with eternal significance. Each act of obedience, each moment of spiritual growth, is a foretaste of the total redemption that awaits us.

We cannot overstate the role of the Holy Spirit in this transformative process. The Spirit empowers, convicts, and sanctifies. Without His work in our hearts, our efforts would be in vain. The Spirit molds, challenges, and comforts us as we navigate the complexities of living a sanctified life in a broken world. This divine guide ensures that our journey is not lonely or aimless but directed toward a glorious end.

As we wrap up this chapter on sanctification, we anticipate the discussions in our final chapter, where we will explore what our full redemption will look like. The Scriptures promise a day when we will be made perfect in holiness, free from the presence of sin, and fully restored in the image of our Creator. This promise is not only our future hope but also our motivation to persevere in the sanctifying work of the Spirit today.

In sum, our daily progress and the ultimate transformation that awaits us mark our journey of sanctification. Each step we take in the Spirit's power is a step closer to our final redemption. Let us then press on, not discouraged by our imperfections but inspired by the complete renewal that will come when we stand in the presence of Christ. As we move toward this conclusion, let us fill our hearts with anticipation and let our lives reflect the transformative work of the Holy Spirit, shaping us ever more into the likeness of Christ until the day of His glorious return.

6

THE GLORIOUS END:

DIVINE ORDER PERFECTED

In our final chapter, "The Glorious End: Divine Order Perfected," we reach the pinnacle of our spiritual journey. This chapter reinforces Christian hope, affirms God's sovereignty, and inspires vivid anticipation of the eternal kingdom. It provides a comprehensive look at the restoration of divine order and our role within it, offering reassurance that every trial and triumph on our earthly path is part of God's grand design. As we explore this chapter, we witness God's promises coming to fruition, with each section thoughtfully arranged to lead you through a narrative of redemption, transformation, and eternal glorification, filling you with awe and wonder.

Sin's Ripple Effect: From Eden to Modern-Day

The biblical narrative of redemption and the ultimate restoration of divine order is deeply intertwined with the profound impact of sin. It's not merely an account of moral failure but a crucial backdrop against which the entire scope of God's redemptive plan unfolds, leading to the Glorious End, where divine order perfects itself.

Genesis 3:17-19 vividly depicts the origin of sin's devastating impact. The consequences of Adam and Eve's disobedience are laid bare: "Cursed is the ground because of you; through painful toil, you will eat food from it all the days of your life. It will produce thorns and thistles for you, and you will eat the plants of the field. By the sweat of your brow, you will eat your food until you return to the ground since from it you were taken; for dust you are, and to dust you will return." This curse illustrates the immediate physical and spiritual ramifications of sin—hardship, pain, and mortality, marking the inception of decay and death into God's perfect creation.

The Apostle Paul, in his epistle to the Romans, delves into the expansion and universal consequences of sin. Romans 5:12 explains, "Therefore, just as sin entered the world through one man, and death through sin, and in this way death came to all people because all sinned." This passage connects the universality of death directly to the universality of sin, underlining that the corruption introduced by Adam has permeated all of creation, affecting every human being.

As Paul continues in Romans 8:22, he notes, "We know that the whole creation has been groaning as in the pains of childbirth right up to the present time." This metaphor suggests suffering, decay, and the anticipatory hope of a new, redeemed order. According to Paul, the entire cosmos is awaiting its liberation from the bondage of corruption—a freedom that will come with the return of Christ and the consummation of God's kingdom.

Romans 3:23 encapsulates humanity's plight under sin: "For all have sinned and fall short of the glory of God." This universal guilt necessitates a universal solution, which we find in the person and work of Jesus Christ. The fall from grace has individual and cosmic consequences, thus setting the stage for cosmic redemption.

The story of sin may seem bleak, but it's not the end. It's a prelude to the unfolding of divine grace that culminates in "The Glorious End: Divine Order Perfected." Here, the narrative shifts from the devastation of sin to the hope of restoration. Christ restores the relationship between God and humanity; all creation will renew itself. The promise of a new heaven and a new earth, where there is no more death, mourning, crying, or pain, fulfills the confident expectation of every Believer. The final chapters of Revelation describe this restoration in vivid detail, assuring us that God will wipe away every tear and death will be no more.

In this final chapter, as we explore the ultimate redemption of creation and the perfection of divine order, we hold fast to the hope that we will completely undo the effects of sin. Through Christ, we look forward to the resurrection, the restoration of our bodies, and our eternal fellowship in the presence of God.

This hope of a new creation, where His perfect order establishes itself, righteousness dwells, and God's glory fully manifests, is not just a distant dream. It sustains, drives, and awaits us, as promised in the Scriptures. This promise is our anchor in the storms of life, our beacon of hope in a world marred by sin, and our assurance of a future free from the shackles of sin.

Hope of Glory: Anticipating Eternal Life with God

In the Christian journey, hope is not just a comforting notion but a vital, animating force—our "Hope of Glory." This anticipation is deeply embedded in the scriptural narrative, promising an eternal life wherein perfect communion with God restores itself, and the scars of sin heal completely.

The Apostle Paul dynamically portrays this hope, extensively mediating its nature and significance. In Romans, he describes salvation shaped by hope for that which we do not see and encourages steadfast patience until its fulfillment.

As Paul articulates in Romans 8:24-25, "For in this hope we were saved. But hope that is seen is no hope at all. Who hopes for what they already have? But if we hope for what we do not yet have, we wait for it patiently." This profound insight suggests that true Christian hope involves waiting with endurance, underpinned by an assured future promised by God.

Hebrews 6:19 vividly describes the imagery of hope as an anchor, which is said to be both "firm and secure." This metaphor powerfully conveys how our hope, linked to Jesus' high priestly ministry, extends into the very presence of God—beyond the veil. It stabilizes our souls amidst life's storms, assuring us of stability and safety provided by God's unchangeable character and His irrevocable promises.

Paul's encouragement in 2 Corinthians 4:17-18 further expands our understanding by calling us to focus on the eternal rather than the transient: "For our light and momentary troubles are achieving an eternal glory that far outweighs them all. So we fix our eyes not on what is seen, but on what is unseen, since what is seen is temporary, but what is unseen is eternal." Here, we contrast the transient nature of our current afflictions with the eternal weight of glory that awaits, framing our trials as preparatory work for an incomprehensible future joy.

Linking this hope directly to the power of the resurrection, 1 Peter 1:3-5 reminds us that we are born into a "living hope through the resurrection of Jesus Christ from the dead." This living hope secures us an imperishable and undefiled inheritance, kept in heaven for us—underscoring that our hope is as alive and active as Christ, who conquered death and guarantees our future resurrection.

Revelation 21:3-4 beautifully illustrates the culmination of this hope, where the final divine promise is unveiled: "And I heard a loud voice from the throne saying, 'Look! God's dwelling place is now among the people, and He will dwell with them. They will be His people, and God will be with them and their God. He will wipe every tear from their eyes. There will be no more death or mourning or crying or pain, for the old order of things has passed away.'" In this promised new creation, the fullness of our hope is realized as God restores everything, eliminating pain, death, and sorrow.

This hope shapes how we live in the present. Romans 12:12 encourages Believers to "Be joyful in hope, patient in affliction, faithful in prayer." These practices reflect a lifestyle oriented towards the future God has promised, influencing our actions and attitudes in the everyday.

Ultimately, the "Hope of Glory" is a transformative expectation. It is not merely about waiting for what will come but actively engaging in a life that mirrors the glorious reality we anticipate. This hope infuses every moment with purpose, guiding us through challenges and enriching our communal and individual experiences with meaning as we look forward to sharing the eternal life promised in God's perfect presence. As we move towards the final consummation, our lives here are lived with a fervent anticipation of that day when we will see God face to face and enter fully into the joy of His kingdom.

Groaning and Awaiting: The Holy Spirit's Role

In the biblical narrative, the themes of groaning and awaiting capture the profound sense of yearning for redemption that permeates humanity and creation. This longing, deeply rooted in the consequences of sin, is vividly portrayed in the Scriptures and highlights the pivotal role of the Holy Spirit in sustaining Believers through these times of expectancy.

Romans 8:22-23 reveals, "We know that the whole creation has been groaning as in the pains of childbirth up to the present time. Not only so, but we, who have the first fruits of the Spirit, groan inwardly as we wait eagerly for our adoption to Sonship, the redemption of our bodies." This passage strikingly illustrates that the groaning is universal, affecting all creation. It likens the anticipation to the pains of childbirth, suggesting that although the present is rife with suffering, it leads to a joyous new beginning. This groaning is a response to current pain and a hopeful one, looking forward to the promised renewal.

Paul further discusses the role of the Holy Spirit in Romans 8:26, stating, "In the same way, the Spirit helps us in our weakness. We do not know what we ought to pray for, but the Spirit Himself intercedes for us through wordless groans." This profound insight into the Spirit's work within us shows that even when our words fail, the Spirit actively communicates our deepest longings and needs to God, aligning our prayers with the Divine will. The Holy Spirit bridges our present experiences and our future hope, ensuring that our groans are not expressions of despair but of anticipation for what is to come.

The groaning extends beyond a personal or isolated experience, as seen in Romans 8:19, "For the creation waits in eager expectation for the children of God to be revealed." This verse emphasizes that creation personifies itself, awaiting the full realization of God's children's glory. This communal aspect of waiting highlights the interconnectedness of God's creation in the redemption narrative.

In 2 Corinthians 5:2-4, Paul elaborates on this theme, "Meanwhile we groan, longing to be clothed instead with our heavenly dwelling, because when we are clothed, we will not be found naked. For while we are in this tent, we groan and are burdened, because we do not wish to be unclothed but to be clothed instead with our heavenly dwelling, so that what is mortal may be swallowed up by life." Here, the clothing metaphor reflects our deep desire to be transformed and to shed our mortality for life eternal, a transformation made possible through Christ's redemptive work.

Jude 1:21 advises Believers to "keep yourselves in God's love as you wait for the mercy of our Lord Jesus Christ to bring you to eternal life." This exhortation encourages Believers to remain steadfast in faith and love during times of waiting, reinforcing the role of active hope in the Christian life.

Therefore, this symphony of groaning and awaiting does not mark itself by passive resignation but by active anticipation facilitated by the Holy Spirit. The Spirit sustains us during these times and actively interprets and elevates our human longings to the Divine, transforming our groans into prayers and our waiting into preparation for revealing the glory.

As we reflect on these Scriptures, it becomes clear that the Holy Spirit is essential in maintaining our focus on the promised end—perfect union with God in a renewed creation. This hope is not confined to the spiritual realm but is a transformative force that impacts how we live in the present, urging us to persevere, pray, and remain firm in our faith. The narrative of groaning and awaiting thus culminates in a glorious anticipation of redemption, where the present pains will give way to the joys of eternal life with God, perfectly restoring the divine order once marred by sin.

The Unseen Intercessors: Spirit and Son at Work

In the rich tapestry of Christian theology, the Trinity encapsulates a profound belief about the nature of God: three distinct persons—God (the Father), Jesus (the Son), and the Spirit (Holy Spirit)—who, though different in personhood, are united in essence. This unity speaks to a perfect and eternal oneness, pivotal for understanding divine intercession dynamics that deeply affect a Believer's spiritual life.

While not termed as such in Scripture, the concept of the Trinity is a cornerstone of Christian doctrine, illustrating that the Father, Son, and Holy Spirit operate in a harmonious unity with distinct roles. Each Person of the Trinity performs unique functions but shares the same divine characteristics, underscoring their perfect unity. This understanding is crucial in comprehending how divine intercession is orchestrated within the Godhead, as each plays a role in the grand narrative of redemption and intercession for humanity.

Romans 8:26-27 captures the Holy Spirit's role in intercession, where Paul writes, "The Spirit (Holy Spirit) helps us in our weakness. We do not know what to pray for, but the Spirit (Holy Spirit) Himself intercedes for us through wordless groans. And He who searches our hearts knows the mind of the Spirit (Holy Spirit) because the Spirit (Holy Spirit) intercedes for God's people in accordance with the will of God (the Father)." This passage highlights the Spirit's intimate involvement in the Believer's life, translating inarticulate human groans into divine petitions that perfectly align with God's (the Father's) will.

Simultaneously, the intercessory role of Jesus (the Son) complements that of the Holy Spirit. Romans 8:34 underscores this dual advocacy, stating, "Who then is the one who condemns? No one. Christ Jesus (the Son) who died—more than that, who was raised to life—is at the right hand of God (the Father) and is also interceding for us." Jesus' (the Son's) advocacy is continuously present in Heavenly. He represents humanity before God (the Father), ensuring that divine mercy and grace are perpetually available to those who believe.

Further, Hebrews 7:25 elaborates on this eternal priesthood of Jesus (the Son): "Therefore He is able to save completely those who come to God (the Father) through Him because He always lives to intercede for them." Here, Jesus' (the Son's) ongoing intercession is vital for the Believer's salvation and continuous sanctification, depicting

Him as an eternal mediator who secures and maintains our standing before God (the Father).

Moreover, Hebrews 9:24 offers insight into the singular nature of Jesus' (the Son's) priestly ministry: "For Christ (the Son) did not enter a sanctuary made with human hands that was only a copy of the true one; He entered heaven itself, now to appear for us in God's (the Father's) presence." Unlike earthly priests, Jesus' (the Son's) ministry directly presents His sacrifice in the heavenly sanctuary, underscoring the completeness and efficacy of His work on our behalf.

Additionally, 1 John 2:1 reaffirms the advocacy role of Jesus (the Son): "My dear children, I write this to you so that you will not sin. But if anybody does sin, we have an advocate with the Father—Jesus Christ (the Son), the Righteous One." This assurance comforts Believers that despite our shortcomings, Christ's (the Son's) righteous advocacy continuously shields us from condemnation.

This symphony of intercessory actions by the Holy Spirit and Jesus (the Son) underlines a broader theological truth about the Trinity. Though their roles in the redemption narrative are distinct, their essence and objectives are harmoniously unified. This divine cooperation ensures that our prayers are heard, refined, and aligned with the divine purpose, reflecting the unified will of the Godhead.

In every prayer and spiritual struggle, this divine fellowship envelops Believers—supported by Jesus' (the Son's) ongoing mediation, the Holy Spirit's deep understanding and translation of our needs, and God's (the Father's) compassionate response.

This theological framework enriches our understanding of prayer and divine interaction, assuring us that our spiritual lives are profoundly supported and sustained within the Trinity's perfect unity. As we navigate our earthly journey, this divine intercession guides us toward the ultimate fulfillment of God's (the Father's) plan, where we will realize the fullness of redemption and perfectly restore divine order.

Events Preceding Christ's Return

In the fabric of Christian eschatology, a series of profound, world-altering events herald the return of Christ, vividly depicted across both the Old and New Testaments. These prophetic scriptures offer Believers crucial markers that help them discern the times and spiritually prepare for the Second Coming. Understanding these prophecies involves recognizing their interconnections and the broader narrative they weave about God's ultimate plan for redemption.

The Gospels present a dramatic and clear description of cosmic disturbances that precede Christ's return. They depict a scene where "the sign of the Son of Man" appears in heaven, and all the peoples of the earth mourn as they see the Son of Man coming on the clouds of heaven with power and great glory.

The angels will be sent out with a loud trumpet call to gather the elect from across the earth (Matthew 24:30-31). This imagery is symbolic and meant to convey the global and unmistakable nature of Christ's return, an event filled with majesty and divine authority.

Paul further elaborates on this moment, describing the Lord's descent from heaven as marked by a loud command, the voice of the archangel, and the trumpet call of God. This event, during which the dead in Christ rise first, marks a triumphant victory over death and signals the resurrection hope clearly (1 Thessalonians 4:16). It is a powerful affirmation of God's sovereignty and the fulfillment of His promises to His people, neither silent nor hidden.

Paul also warns of a period of rebellion and the emergence of a deceptive figure known as the "man of lawlessness," who opposes God. This individual's revelation is a sign of the end times, indicating a significant apostasy and moral decay within humanity (2 Thessalonians 2:3). These warnings are crucial as they provide context for the spiritual landscape before Christ's return, underscoring the need for vigilance and faithfulness among Believers.

In the Old Testament, the prophet Daniel describes a time of distress unmatched by the beginning of nations, coinciding with the deliverance of those whose names appear in the Book of Life. Daniel highlights the severity of this period but also assures that Michael, the great prince who protects God's people, will arise to deliver them from these trials (Daniel 12:1). This prophecy aligns with the New Testament revelations, providing a continuous thread through the scriptures about the trials and ultimate rescue of the faithful.

The Book of Revelation adds to this narrative by depicting the opening of the sixth seal, which brings about cataclysmic changes: a great earthquake, the sun turning black, the moon becoming like blood, and stars falling to the earth. These terrifying and awe-inspiring signs signal the imminent final judgments and underscore the need for repentance and readiness among all people (Revelation 6:12-17).

Together, these prophecies form a comprehensive and cohesive narrative that aims not to incite fear but to prepare and fortify the faith of Believers. They underscore the importance of being spiritually vigilant, keeping faith in God's promises, and living in a manner that reflects readiness for Christ's return. For Christians, these signs are not merely warnings but also affirmations of God's sovereign control over history and His unchanging plan for the redemption of the world. This understanding encourages Believers to face the future with confidence and hope, grounded in the assurance of Christ's imminent return and the glorious restoration that will follow.

Christ's Return: Be Prepared

The return of Christ stands as the pivotal moment in God's redemptive plan, a culminating event eagerly anticipated by Believers throughout the ages. This grand event is not just a future promise but a cornerstone of Christian faith, encapsulated in numerous scriptural passages that describe it in vivid detail. Understanding the significance of Christ's return involves delving into these biblical texts, which comprehensively portray the power and glory that will characterize this divine intervention.

As foretold in 1 Thessalonians 4:16-17, the return of Christ will be a spectacular, supernatural event: "For the Lord Himself will come down from heaven, with a loud command, with the voice of the archangel and with the trumpet call of God, and the dead in Christ will rise first. After that, we who are still alive and are left will be caught up together with them in the clouds to meet the Lord in the air. And so we will be with the Lord forever." This passage highlights the dramatic nature of Christ's return. It reassures Believers of the resurrection and rapture, affirming that all who have died in Christ and those who remain will be united with Him eternally.

The Gospel of Matthew provides additional context, describing the visible signs of Christ's coming. Matthew 24:30 states, "Then the sign of the Son of Man will appear in heaven. And then all the peoples of the earth will mourn when they see the Son of Man coming on the clouds of heaven, with power and great glory." This scripture emphasizes the universal visibility of Christ's return and the mixed reactions it will provoke—mourning for some, indicative of regret or fear, and joyous anticipation for those who have awaited His coming.

Revelation adds a layer of detail to the nature of Christ's return, portraying it as a moment of justice and triumph over evil. Revelation 19:11-16 depicts Christ as a royal conqueror: "I saw heaven standing open and there before me was a white horse, whose rider is called Faithful and True. With justice, he judges and wages war. His eyes are like blazing fire, and his head has many crowns. On his robe and thigh, he has this name written: KING OF KINGS AND LORD OF LORDS." This imagery underscores the authority and majesty of Christ at His return, fulfilling His role as the righteous judge and divine warrior.

Titus 2:13 encourages Believers to live in anticipation of this glorious event: "While we wait for the blessed hope—the appearing of the glory of our great God and Savior, Jesus Christ." This verse calls Christians to a life of godliness and eager expectation, highlighting Christ's return as the blessed hope that motivates ethical and spiritual vigilance.

Acts 1:11 reminds us of the certainty of this event, as angels declared to the disciples after Jesus' ascension: "Men of Galilee," they said, "why do you stand here looking into the sky? This same Jesus, who has been taken from you into heaven, will come back in the same way you have seen Him go into heaven." This assurance links Christ's ascension with His promised return, affirming it as a future reality grounded in historical fact.

Collectively, these scriptures weave a compelling narrative that frames Christ's return as an event to observe and a transformative moment for creation. It marks the end of current worldly suffering and the beginning of eternal fellowship with God. For Christians, this knowledge shapes their worldview and daily conduct, inspiring hope and perseverance amid life's challenges. Believers thus respond by living in readiness, reflecting the hope and purity that anticipate the glorious return of Christ, who will restore all things and reign forever in perfect justice and peace.

Total Transformation: Christ's Complete Glory

The doctrine of our transformation into Christ's image encapsulates a profound hope that defines the Christian journey. It is a promise that stretches from the present reality of our lives, marked by struggles and imperfection, to the glorious future at Christ's return when we will be made perfect and immortal. This transformation, intricately woven through scriptural texts, offers future hope and present help as we navigate the complexities of life in a fallen world.

We find a detailed exposition of this transformative hope in Paul's letters. He explains in 1 Corinthians 15:49 how we, who now bear the image of the earthly man, shall also bear the image of the heavenly man. This statement sets the stage for understanding that just as we have shared in the humanity of Adam, so too will we share in the divinity of Christ, reflecting His glory and purity. It's a powerful promise that our final state will be as gloriously divine as Christ's own resurrected body, free from the corruption of sin.

Paul expands on this concept in Philippians 3:21, where he assures us that Christ will transform our lowly bodies to be like His glorious body. This transformation is rooted in the vastness of Christ's power, the same power He exerts to bring all things under His control. Here, we see the scope of Christ's authority and its impact on Believers—promising a spiritual makeover and a complete physical transformation at the end of the age.

This hope is made even more intimate in 1 John 3:2, where John tells us that though it is not yet clear what we shall be, we can be confident that when Christ appears, we will be like Him, for we shall see Him as He is. This direct encounter with Christ is portrayed as the catalyst for our transformation, implying that our complete conformity to His image will occur in a moment of revelation when we meet Him face-to-face.

Romans 8:29 ties our transformation into the broader narrative of God's redemptive purpose, stating that those God foreknew, He also predestined to be conformed to the image of His Son. This conformity is not just about external resemblance but sharing in the holiness, love, and authority of Christ Himself. It situates our transformation within the vast family of God, where Christ is the Savior and the elder brother, leading many to glory.

Moreover, 2 Corinthians 3:18 clearly illustrates how this transformation is already underway through the work of the Holy Spirit. As Believers, we are transforming into His image with ever-increasing glory, a process that the Spirit initiates and sustains. This verse highlights the progressive nature of our sanctification; even now, we are on a path that bends ever closer to the full likeness of Christ.

This continuous transformation is both a comfort and a challenge. It offers solace by assuring us that our current struggles with sin and mortality are not the end of our story—we are preparing for a glory that far outweighs them. Yet, it also challenges us to live in the light of this coming transformation, to strive for holiness, to nurture our spiritual lives, and to remain steadfast in our faith.

Therefore, as Believers contending with the effects of sin in our mortal bodies, we are encouraged to hold fast to this blessed hope of transformation. Our current experience, with all its trials and imperfections, is a temporary chapter in the grand narrative of our lives. We are moving toward an eternal life that mirrors Christ's perfect and glorified life. Armed with this knowledge, we can face daily challenges with renewed strength and hope, living as citizens of heaven even while we walk the earth. This truth should inspire us to live with purpose and passion as we eagerly await the day when we actively complete our transformation into the image of Christ.

Joint Heirs: Complete Adoption and Sonship

How are we both sons and simultaneously waiting to be adopted as sons?

This question captures the intriguing paradox at the heart of Christian theology concerning our identity in Christ. It highlights the dynamic yet complex nature of our spiritual status, as the New Testament articulates, where Believers already count as children of God yet still anticipate a fuller realization of this Sonship.

The Apostle Paul describes this tension using the metaphor of adoption. Although Jesus has secured redemption for our whole being—spirit, soul, and body—this redemption is only partially realized in our present experience. Our spirits reflect our new identity as God's children, fully renewed, yet we wait for the redemption of our bodies. In 1 John 3:2, John explains that only when we see Christ face-to-face will we be made completely like Him, fulfilling our transformation.

This already-but-not-yet state of adoption is not merely a theological nuance but a practical reality that influences how we live today. While we navigate our earthly lives, contending with sin and its effects, we hold fast to the promise of complete transformation. This promise assures us that our current struggles are temporary and a glorious future awaits where we will fully realize our identity as God's children.

The theological concept of adoption and sonship illustrates the profound transformation Believers undergo as we integrate into God's family. This transformation marks a shift from a mere legal standing to a profoundly relational and eternal bond with God as our Father—a relationship characterized by love, inheritance, and identity as God's children.

Paul's letters to the early churches delve deep into this relationship, particularly emphasizing the transition from fear to freedom. In Romans 8:15-23, he contrasts the spirit of slavery, which leads to fear, with the Spirit of adoption, through which we gain the confidence to call God "Abba, Father." This distinction highlights an intimate relationship with God and signifies our transition from servitude to family.

This theme is further developed in Galatians 4:4-7, where Paul explains how Christ's redemption enables our adoption as sons and daughters. "Because you are His sons, God sent the Spirit of His Son into our hearts, the Spirit who calls out, 'Abba, Father.'" This dynamic indicates that our adoption goes beyond legal rights to a heartfelt recognition of our familial bond with God, brought about by the Holy Spirit who dwells within us.

In Ephesians 1:5, Paul discusses the preordained nature of this relationship, stating that God "predestined us for adoption to sonship through Jesus Christ, in accordance with his pleasure and will." This predestination is not merely about foreknowledge but a deliberate plan of familial inclusion that fulfills God's purpose and pleasure.

John's Gospel affirms the transformational power of belief in Christ in John 1:12, stating, "Yet to all who did receive Him, to those who believed in His name, He gave the right to become Children of God." This passage underscores that our adoption is not based on natural descent or human decision but is rooted in divine action and response to faith.

Finally, Revelation 21:7 vividly portrays the ultimate fulfillment of our Sonship: "Those who are victorious will inherit all this, and I will be their God, and they will be my children." This promise speaks to the inheritance awaiting us and the completed state of our relationship with God in the new creation, where His presence will be our light and His lordship our joy.

These scriptures collectively encourage Believers to embrace fully the identity and privileges of divine Sonship. Knowing that we will transform into God's children helps us live today in light of this future reality. It calls us to live lives marked by godliness as we anticipate the complete realization of our adoption at Christ's return. This doctrinal understanding provides comfort for the present and a profound motivation to live out our faith with anticipation and joy, knowing that the full manifestation of our identity as God's children lies just over the horizon.

New Heaven and New Earth: End of Sin's Effect

In the tapestry of Christian eschatology, the promise of a new heaven and a new earth represents the culmination of God's redemptive plan. In this profound transformation, the scars left by sin are entirely healed. This vision, painted across the scriptures, offers Believers a picture of total renewal— where the very fabric of creation is made pure, and God irrevocably establishes His presence among His people.

The Apostle John in Revelation 21:1-5 provides a glimpse of this majestic renewal. He describes a scene where heaven and earth first pass away, replaced by a new reality free from the former things—pain, mourning, and death have no place. God Himself will dwell with His people, wiping away every tear from their eyes, which signifies God's deep personal relationship with each individual. The declaration that "death shall be no more" promises an existence transcending our current understanding of life, permeated by everlasting peace and joy.

Peter contributes to this vision in 2 Peter 3:13, where he speaks of looking forward to new heavens and a new earth where righteousness is at home. This expectation anticipates a change in physical surroundings and a transformation of the moral landscape. In this new creation, righteousness isn't merely present; it dwells profoundly and permanently, influencing every interaction and relationship.

The detailed imagery continues in Revelation 22:1-5, where the river of the water of life, as clear as crystal, flows from the throne of God and the Lamb down the middle of the city's great street. On each side of the river stands the tree of life, bearing twelve fruit crops and yielding its fruit every month. The tree leaves are for the healing of the nations, suggesting a restoration not only of individual lives but of entire communities and cultures, healing divisions and creating a tapestry of unity and peace.

2 Corinthians 5:17 reflects this reality personally, stating that if anyone is in Christ, he is a new creation; the old has gone, and the new has come. This personal renewal is a microcosm of the cosmic change we anticipate; just as our hearts and minds are made new through Christ, the entire universe will be transformed into a place that perfectly reflects God's glory.

The final removal of sin's effects is perhaps most poignantly described in Revelation 21:4 and Revelation 22:3. The former reassures us that in this new reality, "there will be no more death or mourning or crying or pain," painting a picture of complete and eternal relief from the sufferings that define our current existence. The latter passage promises, "No longer will there be any curse," signifying the total eradication of sin and its consequences. The throne of God and the Lamb will be in the city, and His servants will serve Him, seeing His face and reigning forever and ever. This eternal reign contrasts sharply with earthly rulers' temporary and often tumultuous reigns.

1 Corinthians 15:54-57 celebrates the victory over sin and death, proclaiming, "Death has been swallowed up in victory." This declaration is not just a future hope but a present reality made by Christ's resurrection, which guarantees our victory over death and sin.

Romans 8:21 and Revelation 20:14 further illuminate this theme. Romans promises that "the creation itself will be liberated from its bondage to decay and brought into the glorious freedom of the children of God," indicating a universal liberation from the effects of sin. Revelation depicts the final defeat of death, thrown into the lake of fire, symbolizing the ultimate and irreversible conclusion of sin's reign.

This expansive vision of a new heaven and a new earth, free from sin and its effects, provides hope for the future and a powerful motivation for living today. As we anticipate this glorious transformation, We must live as reflections of this future reality, embodying the values of the Kingdom of God in our daily lives, spreading the message of hope, and actively participating in the preparation for this new creation.

This promise of renewal and restoration is a beacon of hope in a world often darkened by pain and loss. It encourages us to persevere in faith, uplifted by the certainty of God's victory and the sure knowledge that our current struggles with sin and its effects are temporary. The new heaven and new earth await, promising an eternity where God's presence is our light and His peace our perpetual inheritance.

Eternal Worship: The Unceasing Praise in Heaven

In the grand narrative of redemption and divine glory, The culmination of our Christian journey does not mark an end but signals an eternal commencement. In worship, it transforms into an unbroken stream of adoration and praise. As we envision the scenes of heavenly worship, The Scriptures offer us vivid portraits of this divine spectacle, where the glory of God reflects in the ceaseless songs and praises of His creation.

The Book of Revelation, a prophetic manuscript rich with imagery of the last days and the eternal state to come, provides profound insights into what eternal worship entails. In the celestial realms, every creature, every redeemed soul, and all the heavenly hosts come together in a symphony of praise that knows no fatigue or cessation. As Revelation 5:13 poignantly reveals, "Then I heard every creature in heaven and on earth and under the earth and on the sea, and all that is in them, saying: 'To Him who sits on the throne and to the Lamb be praise and honor and glory and power, forever and ever!'" This scripture encapsulates the all-encompassing nature of divine worship that permeates the heavens and the earth.

The unceasing praise in heaven is a testimony to the fulfillment of God's promises and the ultimate defeat of sin. The effects of sin, so palpable and destructive on earth, are nonexistent in heaven. Freed from the shackles of pain, sorrow, and death, the inhabitants of heaven can worship God in a pure and unending manner. This transformation beautifully illustrates itself during the heavenly scene described in Revelation 7:9-12, where a great multitude from every nation, tribe, people, and language stands before the throne and the Lamb. Clothed in white robes and holding palm branches in their hands, they shout with a loud voice: "Salvation belongs to our God, who sits on the throne, and to the Lamb." This passage highlights the diversity of God's kingdom and the unity in worship that transcends earthly divisions.

The continuous praise of God's creatures in heaven further mirrors the activities around the throne, where living creatures never cease to say, "Holy, holy, holy is the Lord God Almighty, who was, and is, and is to come," as chronicled in Revelation 4:8. This repetition, far from being monotonous, underscores the profound truth of God's eternal holiness and sovereign power. These themes are eternally relevant and infinitely profound.

The concept of eternal worship is not confined to the eschatological future but has implications for our worship today. Hebrews 13:15 exhorts, "Through Jesus, therefore, let us continually offer to God a sacrifice of praise—the fruit of lips that openly profess his name." This directive bridges our present experiences with our eternal occupation, suggesting that the praises we offer now foreshadow the eternal praises we will offer in God's unmediated presence. It emphasizes that worship is not episodic but a continual outpouring of our hearts and lives in response to the divine majesty and mercy.

Moreover, the Psalms, especially Psalm 150:6, encapsulate this theme of perpetual praise: "Let everything that has breath praise the Lord. Praise the Lord." This verse serves as a universal call to worship, a command that encompasses all creation, every being that draws breath, in the adoration of the Creator. It highlights the holistic nature of worship, which engages all creation in a chorus of acclaim to the Creator, a foretaste of the heavenly worship that awaits us.

In contemplating these scriptural revelations, we gain a deeper understanding of living in the light of God's eternal glory. The unceasing praise in heaven is not merely an activity but a state of being, a perpetual recognition and celebration of God's sovereignty and love. It is an eternal dialogue of worship, a conversation that began at the dawn of creation and continues throughout eternity, enriched and amplified by every redeemed soul who joins the heavenly chorus.

Thus, as we reflect on "Eternal Worship: The Unceasing Praise in Heaven," we find a conclusion to our earthly journey and an invitation to begin understanding our role in a timeless symphony of praise. This perspective shifts our view from the temporal to the eternal, encouraging us to live lives that reflect our ultimate destiny—worshiping God eternally in a realm where His presence is the light and His glory the air we breathe. As we actively wait to walk out in fullness what is already ours, let us draw near to God, for in the glorious end, the divine order is perfected.

Our praise becomes as ceaseless as His presence. This is the climax of our Christian journey, the moment we join the divine order perfected, singing in eternal harmony with the hosts of heaven, "Glory to God in the highest!" This transcendent celebration, unmarred by the shadows of sin and decay, reflects the ultimate realization of God's plan for His creation. This plan began with creation itself and will culminate into an everlasting, perfect order where His glory manifests in every note sung and every knee bowed.

In this eternal setting, every voice in heaven joins in the anthem of God's redemptive love, encapsulating a profound and unending gratitude. Here, we forever dismantle the barriers that once divided, and the pure essence of God's character is the light that illuminates every corner of the heavenly kingdom. This unity and purity of worship are what we aspire to and what we are moving towards with every day given to us on earth.

This promise of unceasing praise and presence encourages and sustains us through the trials and tribulations of our temporal journey. It is a beacon that guides us, a vision that nurtures our faith, and a powerful reminder that our labor is not in vain. Our weary paths are filled with purpose as we look forward to fully realizing the joy in God's eternal presence.

So let every Believer take heart. Our current challenges and sufferings are but temporary. The celestial worship that awaits us is worth every struggle, a perpetual testament to God's unconditional love for those He has chosen. Let this assurance fill us with joy and an eager anticipation of what is to come, prompting our hearts to cry, "Hallelujah, praise God, and glory to God for His unconditional love!"

As we conclude this chapter, "The Glorious End: Divine Order Perfected," let us cling to this vision of eternal worship. It motivates us to persevere, to continue praising God amidst our current circumstances, and to prepare our hearts for the unending celebration in His presence. This promise propels us forward, the glorious reality that awaits us, and the destiny that every chosen child of God will share—forever singing in perfect harmony, "Glory to God in the highest, forever and ever. Amen."

ABOUT THE AUTHOR

Douglas Mincey, an Ambassador for Christ, is devoted to spreading the message of God's grace through his work as a nonfiction Christian freelance writer. His heartfelt mission is to inspire those in need to find solace and strength in the Lord.

Douglas enjoys reading, watching sports, and exploring new places in his free time. He is married and a proud father of three adult children.

www.ingramcontent.com/pod-product-compliance
Lightning Source LLC
Chambersburg PA
CBHW072126090426

42739CB00012B/3078